SCRIPTURE'S USE OF SCRIPTURE IN THE OLD TESTAMENT

"God's Word often recalls itself within the flow of progressive revelation. This magnificent handbook clarifies the what, how, and why of Old Testament allusions and does so with compelling prose, pedagogical clarity, helpful examples, and faithful interpretation. Swale has created a masterful student manual for interpreting the Old Testament's use of the Old Testament."

—**Jason S. DeRouchie** (PhD, The Southern Baptist Theological Seminary), research professor of Old Testament and biblical theology and Rich and Judy Hastings Endowed Chair of Old Testament Studies at Midwestern Baptist Theological Seminary

"At many points, the Old Testament alludes to other Old Testament texts. With wisdom, insight, and well-chosen examples, Matthew Swale shows us not only how to recognize and evaluate these, but also why they matter. This is a key resource that introduces and explains an important field for reading the Old Testament well while also showing how this is important for how we communicate it in our setting."

—**David G. Firth** (PhD, University of Pretoria), Old Testament tutor at Trinity College Bristol and honorary research associate at the University of the Free State

"Matt Swale offers a fantastic gift to his readers: a book equally learned, accessible, and enriching. *Scripture's Use of Scripture in the Old Testament* gives Marcion a good kick in the knee, and God be praised! Operating with synchronic sensibilities, though alert to diachronic pitfalls, Swale charts a course for identifying allusions in the Old Testament's compositional history. Rich in examples and counterfactual illustrations, Swale's book takes readers on a deep dive into the depths of Scripture's self-awareness and internal conversation. The end result is an Old Testament thick and textured, resplendent in its canonical achievement and life-giving in its revelatory role. If you love Holy Scripture, Swale has left the porch light on and the front door open!"

—**Mark S. Gignilliat** (PhD, University of St. Andrews), professor of divinity (Old Testament) and director of the PhD program at Beeson Divinity School of Samford University

"What an exceptional book! I've waited a long time for a robustly evangelical project on the Old Testament's use of the Old Testament—one that remains accessible yet sophisticated. While there is no shortage of books on the New Testament's use of the Old Testament, resources on the Old Testament's use of the Old Testament are scant. I suspect that professors will require Matthew Swale's volume for their classes, pastors will put it to use for their sermons, and laypeople will learn to use their cross-references. In the end, we will all marvel at the beauty of inner-biblical connections contained therein."

—**Benjamin L. Gladd** (PhD, Wheaton College), executive director of the Carson Center for Theological Renewal at the Gospel Coalition

"Our understanding of how the Old Testament uses the Old Testament has grown considerably in recent years, but scholarship on the topic has remained largely inaccessible to the nonspecialist—that is, until now. Enter Matthew Swale, a reliable and winsome guide on the quest to find allusions within the Old Testament. His *Scripture's Use of Scripture in the Old Testament* offers us key hermeneutical instincts for recognizing, interpreting, and teaching Old Testament allusions, with plenty of helpful examples provided along the way. This practical book is sure to be welcomed by students, teachers, and pastors."

—**Benjamin J. Noonan** (PhD, Hebrew Union College–Jewish Institute of Religion), professor of Old Testament and Hebrew at Columbia International University

"The study of the Bible's use of the Bible finds itself mired in technical language and specialized arguments reserved for academics. Swale masterfully engages with current academic discussions while writing in a friendly voice, engaging both scholars and novices alike. His book offers a helpful introduction to a challenging topic, useful in the classroom and the church."

—**Bryan Murawski** (PhD, Westminster Theological Seminary), associate professor for the School of Divinity at Cairn University

"A dynamic on-ramp! Among the mountains of studies on the Bible's use of the Bible, on-ramps are rare and fun is nonexistent. Matt Swale combines these virtues in *Scripture's Use of Scripture in the Old Testament.* Swale offers practical guidance to help identify, evaluate, and preach scriptural allusions to earlier Scripture. Students and ministers of the Word will benefit from this book's wit and insight."

—**Gary Edward Schnittjer** (PhD, Dallas Theological Seminary), distinguished professor of Old Testament for the School of Divinity at Cairn University

THREE INSTINCTS FOR IDENTIFYING ALLUSIONS

SCRIPTURE'S USE OF SCRIPTURE

IN THE OLD TESTAMENT

MATTHEW E. SWALE

ACADEMIC®
BRENTWOOD, TENNESSEE

Scripture's Use of Scripture in the Old Testament:
Three Instincts for Identifying Allusions
Copyright © 2026 by Matthew E. Swale

Published by B&H Academic®
Brentwood, Tennessee

All rights reserved.

ISBN: 979-8-3845-0023-0

Dewey Decimal Classification: 221.6
Subject Heading: BIBLE. O.T.--CRITICISM, INTERPRETATION, ETC. \ BIBLE. O.T.--STUDY AND TEACHING \ BIBLE. O.T. PSALMS

Unless otherwise indicated, Scripture quotations are taken from The Christian Standard Bible. Copyright © 2017 by Holman Bible Publishers. Used by permission. Christian Standard Bible® and CSB® are federally registered trademarks of Holman Bible Publishers, all rights reserved. Bolded text in the New Testament is used for words quoted directly from the Old Testament.

Scripture marked ESV is taken from The Holy Bible, English Standard Version. ESV® Text Edition: 2016. Copyright © 2001 by Crossway Bibles, a publishing ministry of Good News Publishers.

Scripture marked NIV is taken from Holy Bible, New International Version®, NIV® Copyright © 1973, 1978, 1984, 2011 by Biblica, Inc.® Used by permission. All rights reserved worldwide.

The web addresses referenced in this book were live and correct at the time of the book's publication but may be subject to change.

Cover Design by Mark Karis. Cover illustration from iStock.

Printed in the United States of America

31 30 29 28 27 26 VP 1 2 3 4 5 6 7 8 9 10

To Jackie

טוֹבַת־שֶׂכֶל וִיפַת תֹּאַר

CONTENTS

FOREWORD

Many good academic books and articles devoted to the New Testament's use of the Old Testament have been published over the last century. But in the past decade, several groundbreaking scholars following in the footsteps of Rolf Rendtorff, Brevard Childs, Elmer A. Martens, and others have explored how and why Old Testament writers use Old Testament texts. These efforts have helped us understand, for instance, the many contexts in which later Old Testament authors cite Gen 17:7–8 and Exod 34:5–6. They have also highlighted how lesser-cited texts conveyed God's affirmations and warnings to subsequent generations. Matt Swale's earlier volume on the use of the book of Judges in Psalm 68 is part of this new wave of scholarship.

Now, in this new, engaging, and imaginative book, Swale teaches a much wider audience how to read the Bible as its authors did. He gives appropriate standards for discerning how generations of the Bible's writers benefited from and built on the writings of their predecessors. Swale demonstrates that these writers did not take earlier texts out of context. Thus, he helps us glimpse the process of divine inspiration and human responsibility that 2 Tim 3:14–17 and 2 Peter 1:16–21 describe. Finally, he suggests how we can obey all of God's Word while answering appropriate intellectual questions that careful readers raise. In short, Swale shows us how we can follow the examples of Moses, Isaiah, Huldah, Daniel, and other great Old Testament figures, as Hebrews 11 urges us to do. Managing all this in so few pages is no small achievement, one to celebrate.

What is more, this book helps us follow Jesus's example. Jesus taught that the Old Testament stands for as long as time endures (see Matt 5:17–20). He showed us, his disciples, how to live by its words in our own stressful times.

After all, when hungry, tired, and tempted by Satan, our Lord Jesus Christ recalled what God had told Israel through Moses in Deuteronomy about the purpose of their own time of testing:

> "The whole commandment that I command you today you shall be careful to do, that you may live and multiply, and go in and possess the land that the LORD swore to give to your fathers. And you shall remember the whole way that the LORD your God has led you these forty years in the wilderness, that he might humble you, testing you to know what was in your heart, whether you would keep his commandments or not. And he humbled you and let you hunger and fed you with manna, which you did not know, nor did your fathers know, that he might make you know that man does not live by bread alone, but man lives by every word that comes from the mouth of the LORD." (Deut 8:1–3 ESV)

This passage explains what hardship can teach a follower of the Lord. It stresses the significance of remembering, humbling, knowing, and testing, and it highlights the shaping of a God-oriented heart.

When Satan tested Jesus's heart, pressing him to prove his identity by using his power as God in the flesh to end a God-ordered fast, Jesus responded:

> "Man shall not live by bread alone,
> but by every word that comes from the mouth of God."
> (Matt 4:4 ESV; cf. Luke 4:4 ESV)

He then answered Satan's temptation to test God's love with a quotation from Deut 6:16, and he countered Satan's promise of kingship in exchange for worship by reciting Deut 6:13.

Jesus lived, died, and lived again knowing, quoting, and obeying the Old Testament. Scripture anchored him in his mission by anchoring him in an unshakable relationship with God the Father through the power of God the Spirit. Jesus was a Bible-shaped person.

Ultimately, this book will help you be like Jesus, and nothing matters more than that.

—Paul R. House
Easter 2025

PREFACE

I intend for this book to give advanced undergraduates, seminarians, and pastors a workable method for determining when the Old Testament alludes to another Old Testament text. These concepts are available in scholarly monographs and technical journal articles, but I would like them to be more widely accessible.[1] A recent book expressed the difficulty of making scholarship "accessible to laypeople but still informative for scholars," because "achieving this goal requires delving into some details that may be novel and complex for newcomers (press on!), while avoiding other details that may be expected by specialists (forgive us!)."[2] Nonspecialists may read this book and occasionally think, *Is this section*

---

[1] I hope to offer to the study of the OT use of the OT what Greg Lanier did for the study of the NT use of the OT in *Old Made New: A Guide to the New Testament Use of the Old Testament* (Crossway, 2022), namely, a simple account of a complex scholarly field to make its benefits available to nonspecialists. I developed and used a more technical version of the method outlined in this book in my published dissertation: Matthew E. Swale, *From Recollection to Recommitment: The Rhetorical Function of Allusions to Judges in Psalms 68, 83, and 106*, BBR Dissertation Series 1 (Gorgias, 2024). There, I outline a methodology unique to biblical poetry whereas the methodology here is intended for any OT passage.

[2] Greg Lanier and William A. Ross, *The Septuagint: What It Is and Why It Matters* (Crossway, 2021), 20.

really necessary? Specialists may occasionally think, *Is he really not going to explain Seidel's theory?* To both groups, I apologize in advance for not being the author you dreamed of reading in what I have done and what I have left undone.

If you get hooked on the Old Testament use of the Old Testament, I want to recommend a few works to read next. Any attempt to go further should start with Gary Edward Schnittjer's magnum opus, *Old Testament Use of Old Testament: A Book-by-Book Guide*. Schnittjer is as exhaustive as humanly possible and deftly shows many of the intricate ways the Old Testament uses the Old Testament. If the present work succeeds in its goals, it will equip readers to utilize Schnittjer's more technical book and engage with alluding texts that the scope of his book precludes him from discussing.[3]

I also recommend *Dictionary of the New Testament Use of the Old Testament* (Baker Academic, 2023). This volume was prepared as a companion to its namesake commentary (Baker Academic, 2007). The editors did something brilliant and new here. When they talk about the use of, say, Deuteronomy in the New Testament, they begin by discussing how Deuteronomy uses Scripture and how the Old Testament uses Deuteronomy. If you want to study an Old Testament book's use of

[3] Gary Edward Schnittjer, *Old Testament Use of Old Testament: A Book-by-Book Guide* (Zondervan, 2021), xxii, xix, xvii, xxii, xlvi. Schnittjer covers something many other scholars call inner-biblical exegesis, which he terms "scriptural exegesis of Scripture" (xvii). This refers to alluding texts that "enhance, expand, connect, adjust" their source text (xix). In other words, his aim is not to discuss every allusion in the Old Testament (this would be impossible to do in one book!). At the end of each chapter, he lists additional allusions that do not "enhance, expand, connect, adjust" their source texts. He calls these instances of "broad allusion without interpretation" (xxii). I envision the present work equipping readers to engage Schnittjer's focal texts (inner-biblical exegesis), broad allusions that are listed but not expounded, and allusions he does not detect or address. Schnittjer himself humbly states that "a comprehensive study of all uses of Scripture in Israel's Scriptures is impossible" (xlvi).

Scripture, this would be a wonderful place to start. If you want to learn more about methodology, I recommend starting with Jeffery M. Leonard's excellent article, "Identifying Inner-Biblical Allusions: Psalm 78 as a Test Case" (*JBL*, 2008).

Finally, I apologize in advance for the copious pop culture references that litter the present work. Of course, quotations and allusions do not represent a wholesale endorsement or recommendation of the source material. In my defense, there is a fittingness to including allusions in a book on allusions.

ABBREVIATIONS

BCOTWP	Baker Commentary on the Old Testament Wisdom
BibInt	Biblical Interpretation Series
CBQ	*Catholic Biblical Quarterly*
CJB	Complete Jewish Bible
CTR	*Criswell Theological Review*
EBC	*Expositor's Bible Commentary*
EBTC	Evangelical Biblical Theological Commentary
EHV	Evangelical Heritage Version
FCF	Fallen Condition Focus
FOTL	Forms of Old Testament Literature
GNT	Good News Translation
HALOT	*The Hebrew and Aramaic Lexicon of the Old Testament*
JBL	*Journal of Biblical Literature*
JETS	*Journal of the Evangelical Theological Society*
JSOTSS	Journal for the Study of the Old Testament Supplement Series
KJV	King James Version
LHBOTS	Library of Hebrew Bible/Old Testament Studies
NAC	New American Commentary
NASB	New American Standard Bible

NCBC	New Century Bible Commentary
NCV	New Century Version
NET	New English Translation
NICOT	New International Commentary on the Old Testament
NIVAC	The NIV Application Commentary
NT	New Testament
OT	Old Testament
OTL	Old Testament Library
RCOS	Reformation Commentary on Scripture
RSV	Revised Standard Version
SBJT	*Southern Baptist Journal of Theology*
SJOT	*Scandinavian Journal of the Old Testament*
StBibLit	Studies in Biblical Literature
THOTC	Two Horizons Old Testament Commentary
UBCS	Understanding the Bible Commentary Series
VT	*Vetus Testamentum*
WBC	Word Biblical Commentary
WJK	Westminster John Knox
WTJ	*Westminster Theological Journal*
WYC	Wycliffe Bible
ZECOT	Zondervan Exegetical Commentary on the Old Testament

1

How and Why the Old Testament Uses the Old Testament

Introduction

We parents are no strangers to a children's movie aiming above our kids' pay grade to our own sense of humor or thought world. Sometimes I appreciate being kept in mind, other times I wish they skipped the *entendre*. I won't say which of the two applies to the following example. My sons eagerly awaited the 2022 release of *Sonic the Hedgehog 2*. In a climactic scene, the antagonist—Dr. Robotnik—realizes the protagonist (Sonic) has the upper hand. The antagonist reasons with the protagonist, "What do you say we just let bygones be bygones? I did some things; you did some things. *There are good people on both sides.*"[1]

I immediately realized what my children did not: the filmmaker was not-so-subtly alluding to former President Donald Trump's response to a protest gone awry in 2017. Then-President Trump reportedly said that

[1] *Sonic the Hedgehog 2*, directed by Jeff Fowler (Sony Pictures Entertainment, 2022), 1:44:30–39.

there were "some very fine people on both sides."[2] The allusion revealed the filmmakers' critique of the former president. My kids grasped the scene and its role in the film just fine, but they did not grasp everything the filmmaker sought to communicate.

Judges 19 does something like this in one of the Old Testament's most grim narratives. Two travelers, an unnamed Levite and his concubine, found lodging in the Benjamite city of Gibeah with an unnamed "old man" (v. 16). The city's "wicked men" wanted to mistreat the Levite (vv. 22–23), who sent his concubine out to them instead (v. 25). The Levite used her subsequent mistreatment and resultant death (vv. 25–27) to rally Israel against the city of Gibeah and its tribe (19:29–20:48).

Most readers detect the main point: abandoning Yahweh's governance led to tragic moral, spiritual, and social anarchy in Israel. But like the *Sonic 2* movie quote, the narrator is making an even sharper point than the one that is immediately apparent. The narrator uses six keywords and ten broader plot movements from the infamous Sodom and Gomorrah narrative in Genesis 19.[3] In Genesis 19, people outside the Abrahamic covenant receive judgment because "their sin is extremely serious" (Gen 18:20). What does this add to a Bible reader's understanding of Judges 19's message? Not only did Israel sin, but their sin caused covenantal "deterioration" that rendered them like people who never had the benefit of redemption, covenant, law, and Yahweh's presence.[4] Daniel Block says that Judges traces the "Canaanization" of Israel,[5] and Judges 19 vividly drives home the point

---

[2] Rosie Gray, "Trump Defends White-Nationalist Protesters: 'Some Very Fine People on Both Sides,'" *Atlantic*, August 15, 2017, https://www.theatlantic.com/politics/archive/2017/08/trump-defends-white-nationalist-protesters-some-very-fine-people-on-both-sides/537012/.

[3] The plot similarities and shared terms are listed by Daniel I. Block, *Judges, Ruth*, NAC 6 (B&H, 1999), 519–20.

[4] J. Clinton McCann, *Judges*, Interpretation (WJK, 2002), 115.

[5] Block, *Judges*, 58.

with the allusion: Israelites behave in Judges 19 like those whose evil and distance from God invited his fierce judgment.

Can you understand Judges 19 without noticing and considering the allusion to Genesis 19? Sure. Is the text's message clearer when one follows the reference? Absolutely. This book aims to help people who love the Old Testament to find, follow, and benefit from these references. But why? Why go to the trouble of learning how to track and ruminate on the Old Testament's use of the Old Testament? It's an enchanting thing when we hear about momentous historical figures or celebrities interacting with one another. It's why C. S. Lewis and J. R. R. Tolkien discussing their work over a pint transfixes the imagination. It's why pro boxer Muhammad Ali, human rights activist Malcolm X, football great Jim Brown, and singer-songwriter Sam Cooke hanging out together makes for a fascinating historical fiction premise in *One Night in Miami*. It's why Michael Jordan eulogizing Kobe Bryant, and talking about their wee-hours text threads, is the stuff of hoop fan daydreams. Oh, to be the proverbial fly on those walls. To hear their dialogue. To see their influence on one another.

Readers of the New Testament have long noted its writers' dialogue with the Old Testament. We have learned to be flies on that wall. Michael Graves rightly warns, "It would be unfortunate, however, to overlook the many ways that Scripture interprets Scripture even within the Old Testament."[6] We risk missing the opportunity to see the dialogical interconnectedness of the Old Testament, because it is not always an easy dialogue to notice. Unless we pursue the tools and instincts to be flies on this wall, we will go on hearing from the Old Testament books but miss their intimate dialogue with one another.

Maybe attention to allusions affords us the opportunity to be more than just flies on the wall. Christopher Beetham asks, "Why allude?" I will

---

[6] Michael Graves, *How Scripture Interprets Scripture: What Biblical Writers Can Teach Us about Reading the Bible* (Baker Academic, 2021), 21.

answer this question from a biblical-theological perspective, but Beetham asks the more basic human question: Why does God include the human phenomenon of allusion in his Word? Beetham answers, "Sometimes an author can purposely shape an allusion so that the historical-canonical matrix necessary to grasp it is not readily available to every reader of the text." When a reader grows or reads widely enough in the "historical-canonical matrix" and then "unlocks" the allusion, he or she becomes an "insider" with a stronger connection to the alluding text.[7] If this is the case, then allusions may function in a way similar to the hiddenness of Jesus's parables (e.g., Matt 13:10–17) and display the inexhaustible, bottomless complexity of God's Word. This sounds less like a fly on the wall and more like a seat at the table.

How the Old Testament Uses the Old Testament

When Bible readers think about the New Testament using the Old Testament, what probably comes to mind are those times when the biblical writers signal to the reader that they are quoting the Old Testament by saying something like, "It is written" (e.g., Matt 4:4) or "The Scripture says" (e.g., Rom 10:11). Scholars sometimes call this a **formal quotation** because of the introductory phrase signaling the quotation. The Old Testament does not typically make things that easy on its readers. Instead, Old Testament writers employ allusions to other texts (to be fair, New Testament writers do this too).[8] Biblical **allusions** are brief, intentional, recognizable references

---

[7] Christopher Beetham, "Quotation, Allusion, and Echo," in *Dictionary of the New Testament Use of the Old Testament* (Baker Academic, 2023), 690. Beetham is affirmatively interacting with the work of literary critic William Irwin.

[8] While the most self-evident way the New Testament uses the Old Testament is the formal quotation, New Testament authors also employ quotations without introductory signal phrases and frequent allusions. Counts vary among scholars but, for example, G. K. Beale says that while there are 295 NT quotations of the NT (formal or not), estimates of NT allusions to the OT range

to another biblical text. Quotations happen in the Old Testament too but usually without the formulaic introduction the New Testament often uses.[9] Therefore, in this book, I will often refer to **alluding text** and **source text**. The **alluding text** is the passage that uses another passage, and the **source text** is the passage the alluding text uses. In the opening example, Judges 19 is the alluding text and Genesis 19 is the source text.

If you grew up in a movie-quote family as my wife, Jackie, did, you understand the difference between a quote and an allusion. Her family, the Colliers, almost never announces the source of their allusion. Brief phrases suffice to evoke reminiscent laughter. This was tough on me as a young suitor. When everyone laughed but me, Jackie kindly explained the family's allusions to *While You Were Sleeping*, *The Princess Bride*, or *Nacho Libre*. I wouldn't have minded a more New Testament approach: "As Inigo Montoya quipped in *The Princess Bride* . . ." No such luck. Instead, I watched the movies. I did my homework. I developed my instincts for recognizing cinematic allusions (and even still, I often need to ask what movie is being referenced). But it helped me to learn *why* the Colliers loved movie references. I suspect it was a way both to conjure meaningful family memories and cleverly punctuate their conversations. Likewise, to develop an instinct for tracking and interpreting Old Testament allusions, it helps to know *why* Old Testament writers allude to other texts.

While Old Testament writers' reasons for alluding to another text are nearly as diverse as the number of texts that employ allusions, the

---

from 600 to 4,100. G. K. Beale, *Handbook on the New Testament Use of the Old Testament: Exegesis and Interpretation* (Baker Academic, 2012), 58.

[9] There are notable exceptions to this statement. For example, Jer 26:18–19 formulaically introduces a quote from Mic 3:12. Kevin Spawn explains that post-exilic authors like those of Ezra–Nehemiah and Chronicles use citation formulae, like Ezra 3:2's "as it is written in the law of Moses," "to cultivate the responsible handling of the law in the reconstruction era." Kevin Spawn, *"As It Is Written" and Other Citation Formulae in the Old Testament: Their Use, Development, Syntax, and Significance* (de Gruyter, 2002), 257.

following seven general goals emerge: progression, perpetuation, pattern, parallel, punch, prayer, and principle.[10] Those who have studied the New Testament use of the Old Testament may notice a missing "P" in this list: prediction (New Testament writers quoting or alluding to predictive OT texts).[11] Old Testament writers allude to earlier predictive Scripture too, but not nearly as often as does the New Testament.[12] The Old Testament contains predictions aplenty but not as many Old Testament writers refer to predictive texts as do New Testament writers.[13]

One major exception to this statement occurs when an Old Testament passage alludes to Deuteronomy 28 to explain why Israel will soon experience physical adversity. Deuteronomy 28 contains a list of covenant

---

[10] I considered including an eighth "P," but its specialization and diverse rhetorical aims make it less fit for an overview like the present list. However, motivated readers may find the phenomenon of *parody* worth investigating. Will Kynes notes that while some scholars see parodic allusions in the Old Testament to another Old Testament as *targeting* or *subverting* the source text, it is better to see the alluding text as *weaponizing* the earlier text for a variety of rhetorical purposes. For example, he argues that Joel 3:10 alludes to Isa 2:4 as a parody meant to mock the nations and Job 7:17–18 allude to Ps 8:5 as a parody meant to persuade God to treat Job mercifully. The difference in rhetorical purposes in those two examples alone make this a category of allusion that could fit in various places in the list below. Joel's parody is like the *punch* category below, whereas Job's parody is more like the *perpetuation* category below. Will Kynes, "Beat Your Parodies into Swords, and Your Parodied Books into Spears: A New Paradigm for Parody in the Hebrew Bible," *Biblical Interpretation* 19 (2011): 276, 306, 309. For a brief popular-level introduction to parody in Job, see Bill Kynes and Will Kynes, *Wrestling with Job: Defiant Faith in the Face of Suffering* (IVP Academic, 2022), 106–108.

[11] For example, Greg Lanier lists three ways the New Testament uses the Old Testament: prediction, patterns, and prescriptions. His excellent work seems to have subconsciously influenced my own "P" alliteration. Lanier, *Old Made New: A Guide to the New Testament Use of the Old Testament* (Crossway, 2022), 35–37.

[12] For example, Daniel refers to Jeremiah's seventy-year exile prediction (Dan 9:2; Jer 29:10).

[13] The long-range arc of messianic predictions presents one factor in this difference between the use of Scripture in the Old and New Testaments (cf. 1 Pet 1:10–11).

blessings and curses: tangible blessings for trusting and obeying Yahweh (vv. 1–14), and tangible curses for not (vv. 15–68). For example, when Malachi's famous tithe passage says, "You are suffering under a curse, yet you—the whole nation—are still robbing me" (Mal 3:9), Malachi, writes Andrew E. Hill, "is equating the experience of post-exilic Judah with 'the curse' of the Mosaic covenant (cf. Deut 28:20, 27)."[14] This is not a simple one-to-one prediction and fulfillment, however, because many prophets use Deuteronomy 28 in this way, applying its truth to myriad circumstances. Therefore, this instinct probably fits better into one or more of the following categories (perhaps *parallels* or *perpetuation*) than in the category of prediction.

1) Progression

Old Testament writers sometimes use another biblical text to convey a *progression*, or development, in God's interaction with his people. In theological terms, these allusions facilitate a wider concept known as *progressive revelation*. In progressive revelation, God unveils his truth and promises little by little throughout redemptive history. For example, Old Testament saints knew less about the afterlife (e.g., Ps 115:17) than the Holy Spirit would reveal in the New Testament writings (1 Cor 15:12–58). They were not misinformed, but they resided earlier in the gradual process of God unveiling his truth and promises. How does this relate to Old Testament allusions? Old Testament writers referring to prior revelation effectively say: *Remember when God said or did* this*? That's still on the table, but now he is also saying and doing* this.

Second Samuel 7, famous for Yahweh's covenant promises to David, communicates progression by alluding to an earlier moment in redemptive history. Notice the similar words in these two texts:

---

[14] Andrew E. Hill, *Haggai, Zechariah, and Malachi: An Introduction and Commentary*, TOTC 28 (InterVarsity, 2012), 347.

2 Samuel 7:8–9 ALLUDING TEXT	Genesis 12:1–3 SOURCE TEXT
So now this is what you are to say to my servant David: "This is what the Lord of Armies says: I took you from the pasture, from tending the flock, to be ruler over my people Israel. I have been with you wherever you have gone, and I have destroyed all your enemies before you. I will make a great name for you like that of the greatest on the earth."	The Lord said to Abram: "Go from your land, your relatives, and your father's house to the land that I will show you. I will make you into a great nation, I will bless you, I will make your name great, and you will be a blessing. I will bless those who bless you, I will curse anyone who treats you with contempt, and all the peoples on earth will be blessed through you."

In addition to 2 Sam 7:9 "echoing the language of the covenantal promise to Abraham in Genesis 12:2,"[15] the wider contexts of each passage share an impressive number of themes.[16] Shared themes, the subject of chapter 4, heighten the probability of an allusion by demonstrating that the alluding writer addressed matters that may have caused them to recall the source text.

Why would the writer of Samuel allude to Genesis 12 here (i.e., the topic in chapter 5)? David suggests the connection when he says, "This is a revelation for mankind" (2 Sam 7:19b). David grasped that Yahweh's promise—"your throne will be established forever" (v. 16)—presented

[15] Craig E. Morrison, *2 Samuel*, ed. Jerome T. Walsh, Berit Olam (Liturgical Press, 2013), 100.

[16] I detect seven shared themes: (1) the command to "go" (2 Sam 7:3, 5; Gen 12:1), (2) Egypt (2 Sam 7:6; Gen 12:10), (3) a land for dwelling (2 Sam 7:10; Gen 12:7), (4) Yahweh dealing with the subject's enemies (2 Sam 7:1, 11; Gen 12:3), (5) offspring (2 Sam 7:12; Gen 12:7), (6) blessing (2 Sam 7:29; Gen 12:2–3), and (7) global relevance of promises (2 Sam 7:19; Gen 12:3). The seventh theme is more self-evident in the ESV's "this is instruction for mankind" than the NIV's "this decree . . . is for a mere human."

good news not only for him but for all humanity. The allusion to Gen 12:2 clarifies that the promise to Abraham that "all the peoples on earth will be blessed through you" (v. 3) now meant *through* David's royal bloodline.[17] For David, and for Israel, this was new information. Progression. This allusion first unveils the progression from Abraham to David that opens the New Testament: "An account of the genealogy of Jesus Christ, the Son of David, the Son of Abraham" (Matt 1:1).

2) Perpetuation

Old Testament writers sometimes employ another biblical text to connote the *perpetuation*, or continuity, of a prior reality. Whereas the first purpose (progression) communicates new elements in Yahweh's dealings with his people, here Old Testament writers communicate the opposite: the Lord's prior manner of interacting with his people remains in effect. This finds a modern parallel in a recurring theme in African American Christian reflection. The late James Earl Massey argued that the spirituals confess God's ability to do *again* what was done *before*. He illustrates this confession in the song "Didn't My Lord Deliver Daniel?" In this spiritual, the lyricist asks rhetorically why God would not do again for believers what he did when he delivered the likes of Daniel, Shadrach, Meshach, Abednego, and Jonah.[18]

---

[17] Walter Kaiser Jr. argues this point persuasively, adding that 2 Samuel 7's repeated "LORD God" (lit., Adonai Yahweh; vv. 18, 19, 22, 28, 29) is not characteristic of 2 Samuel, but it occurs in the Abraham narrative (Gen 15:2, 8). This divine title heightens the probability both of an allusion to Abrahamic promises and to a development of the global implications of the Abrahamic promises. Walter C. Kaiser Jr., *The Messiah in the Old Testament*, Studies in Old Testament Biblical Theology (Zondervan, 1995), 79–81.

[18] See James Earl Massey, "The African-American Spirituals: Faith and Worship," *Views from the Mountain: Select Writings from James Earl Massey* (Aldersgate, 2018), 121.

Psalm 68:1 offers a clear example of this purpose. Notice the similar words in David's opening confession and Num 10:35:

Psalm 68:1 **ALLUDING TEXT**	**Numbers 10:35** **SOURCE TEXT**
God arises. His enemies scatter, and those who hate him flee from his presence.	Whenever the ark set out, Moses would say: "Arise, Lord! Let your enemies be scattered, and those who hate you flee from your presence."

The psalmist only changes the title for God and the pronouns referring to him, so this may be more of an adapted quote than an allusion.[19] The texts also have five themes in common.[20] Why, then, does David open the psalm with Moses's prayer for moving the ark? John Calvin argues that David expresses "delight" that what Moses prayed for, David himself "saw daily fulfilled before his own eyes."[21] In other words, David communicates through this allusion the *perpetuation* in his own day of how God helped the wilderness generation.

3) Patterns

Old Testament writers employ scriptural allusions to demonstrate *patterns* in the biblical storyline. Theologians call this phenomenon *typology*,

[19] Marvin E. Tate, *Psalms 51–100,* 2nd ed., WBC 20 (Zondervan, 2018), 175.

[20] Both texts address: (1) traveling or transition (Ps 68:6; Num 10:35), (2) wilderness or desert (Ps 68:7; Num 10:31), (3) movement from Sinai (Ps 68:17; Num 10:12), (4) references to multitudes (Ps 68:17; Num 10:36), and (5) God's discipline (Ps 68:2, 6; Num 11:1). The reference to Sinai is significant in that the word occurs outside of the Pentateuch only in Ps 68:1 and Neh 9:17.

[21] John Calvin, *Commentary on the Book of Psalms*, vol. 3, trans. James Anderson (Logos Bible Software, 2010), 7.

or the establishment of a pattern (type) and its recurrence later (antitype). G. K. Beale defines typology as "correspondences among revealed truths about persons, events, institutions, and other things with the historical framework of God's special revelation, which, from a retrospective view, are of a prophetic nature and are escalated in their meaning."[22] One of the most often referenced typological events in the Old Testament is the exodus. Especially in the prophetic books, biblical writers explain Yahweh's ongoing redemptive activity in terms of *correspondence* with his intervention in the exodus.

For example, notice the similarity between these two texts and its relevance to the patterns in the Old Testament (i.e., typology):

Micah 7:19 ALLUDING TEXT	Exodus 15:1, 5 SOURCE TEXT
He will again have compassion on us; he will vanquish our iniquities. You will cast all our sins <u>into</u> the <u>depths</u> of <u>the sea</u>.	Then Moses and the Israelites sang this song to the Lord. They said: "I will sing to the Lord, for he is highly exalted; he has thrown the horse and its rider <u>into the sea</u>. . . . The floods covered them; they sank to the <u>depths</u> like a stone."

[22] Beale, *Handbook on the New Testament*, 14. Here Beale lists five "essential characteristics" of typology: "(1) analogical correspondence, (2) historicity, (3) a pointing-forwardness (i.e, an aspect of foreshadowing or presignification), (4) escalation, and (5) retrospection." Beale, 14. Recently, James M. Hamilton Jr. has defined typology as "God-ordained, author-intended historical correspondence and escalation in significance between people, events, and institutions across the Bible's redemptive-historical story (i.e., in covenantal contexts)"; he presents two categories of characteristic features: (1) "historical correspondence" (indicated by "key terms," "quotations," "repetitions of sequences of events," and "similarity in salvation-historical or covenantal import") and (2) "escalation in significance" based on the features of historical correspondence. James M. Hamilton Jr., *Typology: Understanding the Bible's Promise-Shaped Patterns* (Zondervan Academic, 2022), 25–26.

Though they show a less impressive overlap than other allusions detailed in this chapter,[23] the two contexts also have several themes in common.[24] Micah vivifies his prediction of future atonement by showing its continuity with the paradigmatic redemptive event in Israel's life and history. The exodus redemption possesses a forward-looking pattern with a view toward a deeper, better redemption from sin. What better way to make this point than to allude to the text that sang about the type (deliverance from slavery) while attempting to teach about the antitype (deliverance from sin)?

4) Parallels[25]

The fourth goal for Old Testament allusions brings to mind an old maxim: "History doesn't repeat itself, but it does rhyme." Sometimes, biblical writers notice parallels between another scriptural text and their present moment and express them to warn the people of God. It is usually

---

[23] Gary Edward Schnittjer explains that the strongest verbal link is the Hebrew word for *depths* used in Mic 7:19 and Exod 15:5, but the tossing and sea imagery is rooted in Exod 15:1. Schnittjer, *Old Testament Use*, 416.

[24] Schnittjer lists seven themes: (1) salvation (Exod 15:2; Mic 7:7), (2) covering (Exod 15:5; Mic 7:10), (3) inheritance (Exod 15:17; Mic 7:14), (4) signs or miracles (Exod 15:11; Mic 7:15), (5) trembling (Exod 15:14; Mic 7:17), (6) loyal love (Exod 15:13; Mic 7:18), and (7) asking, Who is like you? Schnittjer, *Old Testament Use*, 415n12. He draws the list from Lesley DiFransico, "'He Will Cast Their Sins into the Depths of the Sea . . .' Exodus Allusions and the Personification of Sin in Micah 7:7–20," *VT* 67, no. 2 (2017): 192–93.

[25] I do not mean mere similarities between biblical texts, or parallel passages that contain the same or similar material, but I refer to (often negative) parallels highlighted to jolt the audience. For a sad example of how drawing attention to parallels can pack rhetorical force, think of how marriage counselors discourage negatively comparing one's spouse to his or her parents. It will not likely be received as a general, nonrhetorical observation!

not a compliment. The example that began this chapter—Judges 19 and Genesis 19—illustrates this fourth purpose. By demonstrating a parallel between his narration and a prior biblical event, the depth of Israel's sin—and mostly its effects on Israel—become starker. Psalm 106 provides another example of this *parallel* phenomenon. The psalmist moves beyond mere allusion and presents a full-blown recap of the exodus and failures surrounding it (vv. 7–22), failures in the wilderness (vv. 23–33), and failures in the era of judges (vv. 34–46). Why is the psalmist alluding to these broad strokes in Israel's scriptural history? He tells us: "We sinned with our fathers" (v. 6, author's translation). Zinger. He intercedes and calls for repentance by showing a *parallel* between his community's sins and Israel's sins in the past.

5) Punch

A fifth purpose for Old Testament writers to allude to another Old Testament text can coexist with the other purposes. It is also something we do today. We allude in conversation to add *punch*, or rhetorical weight, to a statement. While talking to teenagers, alluding to certain musicians adds punch to a statement (or makes you look ancient). Talking about film, alluding to certain directors or actors adds punch to a statement. Talking about racism, alluding to certain historical figures adds punch to a statement. Old Testament allusions add punch to a biblical text too.

Allusions, especially to formative or infamous texts, add rhetorical *punch* to biblical pronouncements. Jeremiah 4:23 accomplishes this with the underlined allusion to Gen 1:2 (notice the earth, heavens, and light themes Jeremiah employs too):[26]

[26] See Robert P. Carroll, *Jeremiah: A Commentary*, OTL (WJK, 1986), 169.

Jeremiah 4:23 ALLUDING TEXT	Genesis 1:2 SOURCE TEXT
I looked at the earth, and it was formless and empty. I looked to the heavens, and their light was gone.	Now the earth was formless and empty, darkness covered the surface of the watery depths, and the Spirit of God was hovering over the surface of the waters.

In context, Jeremiah announces the coming destruction of Jerusalem (4:22, 27). Prophets paint pictures of future judgment in many ways: agricultural imagery (Isa 5:6), insect imagery (Joel 2:25), animal imagery (Amos 5:19), storm imagery (Jer 23:19), fire imagery (Joel 1:19–20), and more. Here, though, Jeremiah paints a chilling picture of the reversal of creation: because Judah has rejected the author of order and life, God will become to them the "destroyer of order and life."[27] Each prophetic image packs its own force, but employing Israel's own Scripture does so uniquely and sharply.

6) Prayer

Sixth, Old Testament writers allude to other biblical texts in their *prayers*. Jesus prayed Scripture (e.g., Matt 27:46), as did the early church (e.g., Acts 4:23–31). However, Old Testament writers did this first. The most well-known place where biblical writers use Scripture to form and animate their dialogue with God is in the Psalms (e.g., 8; 89; 105–106; 136). For a lesser-known example, consider how Habakkuk prays this way. In the most famous part of his climactic prayer, he animates his prayer with a text from Israel's past:[28]

---

[27] Carroll, *Jeremiah*, 168.

[28] Scripture infuses Habakkuk's prayer beyond this example. Carl E. Armerding argues that Habakkuk 3 bears an "allusive" relationship to Psalm 77, Psalm 18,

Habakkuk 3:19 ALLUDING TEXT	Psalm 18:32–33 SOURCE TEXT
The Lord my Lord is my strength; he makes my feet like those of a deer and enables me to walk on the mountain heights!	God—he clothes me with strength and makes my way perfect. He makes my feet like the feet of a deer and sets me securely on the heights.[29]

Psalms 18:32–33 possesses a beautiful irony.[30] According to the superscription of Psalm 18, David "spoke" that chapter "on the day the Lord rescued him from the grasp of all his enemies." Habakkuk spoke his "prayer" (Hab 3:1) shortly after offering a "complaint" to Yahweh (2:1) that Judah's enemies would conquer them (1:5–11) because of their covenant breaking (1:1–4). But he believed the same strength David found in prayer was available to him, albeit in vastly different circumstances. In fact, Habakkuk may have selected Psalm 18, a Davidic psalm, as a nod to the fact that even Judah's judgment at the hands of Babylon would not end David's line. Habakkuk's generation would deteriorate (Hab 3:17), but the Davidic promises would not, and therefore Judah would survive until Yahweh's glory one day fills the earth (2:14). Schnittjer argues similarly and concludes, "Habakkuk's confidence is grounded upon scriptural testimony to the power of Yahweh."[31]

Deuteronomy 33, and Psalm 68 (in the order of prominence). "Habakkuk," *EBC* 7 (Zondervan, 1985), 520–21. Kevin Chen adds Deuteronomy 32 to the texts Habakkuk 3 uses. Kevin Chen, *Wonders from Your Law: Nexus Passages and the Promise of an Exegetical Intertextual Old Testament Theology* (IVP Academic, 2024), 163–65.

[29] "The heights" (Ps 18:33) and "mountain heights" (Hab 3:19) represent the same Hebrew word.

[30] A parallel version of this prayer exists in 2 Samuel 22, but it is easier to conceive of Habakkuk having access to Psalm 18 than 2 Samuel.

[31] Schnittjer, *Old Testament Use*, 429.

7) Principle

Seventh, sometimes biblical writers allude to an ethical *principle*—usually from the Mosaic law—to explain something in their narrative or their era. For example, in 2 Samuel 12, the prophet Nathan elicits David's repentance for adultery and murder with a parable about a rich man stealing the "ewe lamb" of a poor man (vv. 1–4). David's reply alludes to case law in Exodus:

2 Samuel 12:6 ALLUDING TEXT	Exodus 22:1 SOURCE TEXT
Because he has done this thing and shown no pity, he must pay four lambs for that lamb.	When a man steals an ox or a sheep and butchers it or sells it, he must repay five cattle for the ox or four sheep for the sheep.[32]

There are only three verses in the Old Testament where this word for payment is used with the word *four*: Exod 22:1, 2 Sam 12:6, and 2 Sam 15:7 (where *four* refers to years and *pay* refers to vows). David alludes to a legal *principle* in the law of Moses because he knows it well. Nathan's parable could not have been more successful, because he goaded David to apply Mosaic law to someone else when he had not done so concerning his own sin.

---

[32] Readers may wonder why "lamb" and "sheep" are not underlined here. While they constitute a shared theme (see chapter 4) that confirms the allusion, different Hebrew words are used to describe the animals in these texts. Nathan's parable uses a Hebrew word for *ewe lamb* (2 Sam 12:3), whereas Exod 22:1 uses the more general word for sheep. The word for "ewe lamb" is not common in the Old Testament (8x), but it occurs in the context of sacrificial cleansing in Lev 14:10. Craig Morrison suggests, because of David's subsequent acts of cleansing matching Leviticus 14's prescriptions, that "the 'ewe lamb' in Nathan's parable, a sacrificial animal of expiation, foreshadows David's eventual atonement for his crimes against Uriah." Morrison, *2 Samuel*, 152. Perhaps, then, Nathan too is alluding to a biblical *principle* here.

Again, Old Testament writers allude to Scripture for diverse and intricate reasons. The seven uses listed above, however, account for a great many of them: progression, perpetuation, patterns, parallels, punch, prayer, and principle.

Why Study the Old Testament Use of the Old Testament

Why is it a worthwhile venture not simply to read the Old Testament but also to consider the ways Old Testament texts read other Old Testament texts? In my experience, there are at least three benefits. Considering allusions often clarifies the *meaning* of a biblical text, enables the reader to grasp and adopt the *mindset* of the biblical writers, and demonstrates the interconnected *metanarrative* of the Old Testament.

1) Meaning

If you are reading this book, you are probably also the kind of person who appreciates a good Bible commentary. Commentaries, at their best, help us see what biblical texts mean by *commenting* on those texts. But no commentary does so perfectly (that's why, in my opinion, we must have several). Biblical allusions offer God's people *inspired* and therefore *perfect* comments and perspectives on the source text.[33]

For example, Bible students have long puzzled over God's command to King Saul to "not spare" the Amalekites, including "men and women, infants and nursing babies, oxen and sheep, camels and donkeys" (1 Sam 15:3). King Saul, of course, invites Yahweh's discipline and rejection (v. 23) by sparing someone or something from each commanded category

[33] In a symbiotic interpretive relationship, the alluding text becomes clearer when interpreters consider what they are doing with the source text.

(vv. 8–9). Most notably, he spares the Amalekite King Agag (vv. 32–33). To modern readers (and apparently rabbinic ones too),[34] the initial command appears unnecessarily macabre.

Another biblical writer's use of this text does not answer every modern question, but it at least provides an ancient rationale for Yahweh's command. Look at the names shared in these two texts:

Esther 2:5; 3:1a ALLUDING TEXT	1 Samuel 9:1–2a; 15:8–9a SOURCE TEXT
In the fortress of Susa, there was a Jewish man named Mordecai son of Jair, son of Shimei, son of Kish, a Benjaminite. . . . After all this took place, King Ahasuerus honored Haman, son of Hammedatha the Agagite.	There was a prominent man of Benjamin named Kish son of Abiel, son of Zeror, son of Becorath, son of Aphiah, son of a Benjaminite. He had a son named Saul. . . . He captured King Agag of Amalek alive, but he completely destroyed all the rest of the people with the sword. Saul and the troops spared Agag.

The book of Esther's "darkly foreboding" reference infuses the conflict between Mordecai and Haman with centuries-old drama reaching back even before King Saul's reign (e.g., Exod 17:9; Deut 25:17).[35] However, the allusion also clarifies the intensity of Yahweh's command in 1 Samuel 15. Saul's disobedience left Amalekites, and presumably relatives of Agag, alive. Subsequently, according to authors Robert L. Hubbard Jr. and J. Andrew Dearman, the conflict "fuels the later hatred against Jews by Haman, a descendant of Agag, in the book of

[34] Hanna Liss, "The Innocent King: Saul in Rabbinic Exegesis," *Saul in Story and Tradition*, Forschungen zum Alten Testament 47 (Mohr Siebeck, 2006), 247–48.

[35] Anthony Tomasino, *Esther*, Evangelical Exegetical Commentary (Lexham, 2016), 214.

Esther."[36] King Saul's unfinished business left room for a blood feud that threatened his kin centuries later, a possibility that could have been avoided through trust and obedience to a difficult command.

2) Mindset

What is the goal of Bible reading? We might state this variously. One worthwhile goal that could be called the goal of all evangelical biblical theology is voiced by James M. Hamilton Jr.: "My goal is for the worldview of the biblical authors to be my worldview."[37] Like it or not, our theological worldview is not automatically aligned with the Bible's. Allusions in the Old Testament allow Bible readers to trace the themes that dominated the biblical writers' theological worldview. When I ask my students what God is like, it's not that they're wrong, but their answers lack thickness. *Loving. Father. Savior. Good.* These are not bad answers, and I would never disparage them. But if you asked Moses, he would say, "The Lord is slow to anger and abounding in faithful love, forgiving iniquity and rebellion. But he will not leave the guilty unpunished, bringing the consequences of the fathers' iniquity on the children to the third and fourth generation" (Num 14:18). If you asked Jonah, he would say, "A gracious and compassionate God, slow to anger, abounding in faithful love, and one who relents from sending disaster" (Jonah 4:2).[38] If you

---

[36] Robert L. Hubbard Jr. and J. Andrew Dearman, *Introducing the Old Testament* (Eerdmans, 2018), 160. The allusion in Esther can be interpreted as an "archetypal" and not literal-genealogical reference to the Agag of 1 Samuel 15 (e.g., Andrew J. Schmutzer, "Esther," in *Ezra, Nehemiah and Esther*, Teach the Text Commentary ([Baker Academic, 2018], 239). However, the genealogical interpretation presented here is an old one; see Josephus, *Ant.* 11.209. Moore lists additional sources: the Talmud, the Targums, and "most commentators, who rightly view Haman as a descendant of the Amalekites." Carey A. Moore, *Esther*, Anchor Bible 7B (Doubleday, 1971), 35.

[37] James M. Hamilton Jr., *Psalms*, vol. 1, EBTC (Lexham, 2021), 21.

[38] In an ironic twist, Jonah lists these attributes as a complaint!

asked David, he would say, "A compassionate and gracious God, slow to anger and abounding in faithful love and truth" (Ps 86:15).

These examples span the three traditional Hebrew sections of the Old Testament: the Law, the Prophets, and the Writings. And they only scratch the surface of biblical writers that give this same answer.[39] Why? Because at Israel's covenantal inception Yahweh revealed himself to Moses in these terms:

> The Lord passed in front of him and proclaimed: The Lord—the Lord is a compassionate and gracious God, slow to anger and abounding in faithful love and truth, maintaining faithful love to a thousand generations, forgiving iniquity, rebellion, and sin. But he will not leave the guilty unpunished, bringing the consequences of the fathers' iniquity on the children and grandchildren to the third and fourth generation. (Exod 34:6–7)

Paul R. House rightly states, "Perhaps no better summation of Yahweh's true nature appears in the Old Testament."[40] Old Testament writers agree. Attending to their use of Exod 34:6–7 demonstrates how seminal a statement it makes about God, and allows us to align our *mindset*, our worldview, with that of the Bible.

3) Metanarrative

The 2019 film *Doctor Sleep* is a sequel to the 1980 film *The Shining*. However, none of the original actors recur in leading roles. There is no

---

[39] Hamilton includes Deut 5:9–11; 7:9–10; Isa 63:7; Jer 32:18; Hos 2:19–20; Joel 2:13; Mic 7:18; Nah 1:2–3; Pss 103:8; 111:14; 145:8; Neh 9:17, 31–32. He lists an additional eleven texts that he calls "less certain allusions" to Exod 34:6–7. James M. Hamilton Jr., *God's Glory in Salvation Through Judgment: A Biblical Theology* (Crossway, 2010), 134–37.

[40] Paul R. House, *Old Testament Theology* (InterVarsity, 1998), 123.

Jack Nicholson, and now Ewan McGregor takes centerstage. How does a sequel with none of the same leading actors communicate to its audience that it exists in continuity with an earlier installment? Themes (e.g., alcoholism). Words (e.g., *REDRUM*). Allusions to the first film—both overt (e.g., the creepy twins) and subtle (e.g., room numbers from the Overlook Hotel). Despite the decades between the films, *Doctor Sleep* uses "plenty of flashbacks" to *The Shining* and thus "pays tribute" to the beloved horror flick.[41] How do biblical texts—separated sometimes by centuries, with different main characters, and often different genres—demonstrate their continuity with earlier divine revelation? Themes. Phrases. Allusions to earlier texts. Readers paying attention to these connections receive a payoff: grasping the metanarrative, or the united storyline, of the Bible.

All Old Testament prophets want to communicate a basic message: God's people have *sinned*, unrepentance invites *punishment*, but God graciously makes *restoration* available.[42] Isaiah wants to show that his message of restoration is a sequel to an earlier redemptive episode: the exodus.[43] But Moses isn't alive in Isaiah's day. Neither is Aaron. Isaiah writes poetic, oracular literature, not the narrative or legal material of Exodus. How will Isaiah alert readers that the coming restoration will be a sequel to the exodus without the same characters or even literary forms? He does so like this:

---

[41] Samuel Spencer, "'Doctor Sleep': All the References to 'The Shining' Explained," *Newsweek*, November 8, 2019, https://www.newsweek.com/doctor-sleep-movie-shining-references-easter-eggs-stephen-king-stanley-kubrick-1470166.

[42] Paul R. House and Eric Mitchell, *Old Testament Survey*, 2nd ed. (B&H Academic, 2007), 175.

[43] Scholars call this the Isaianic New Exodus theme. See, for example, Bryan D. Estelle, *Echoes of Exodus: Tracing a Biblical Motif* (InterVarsity, 2018), 149.

ALLUDING TEXTS in Isaiah	SOURCE TEXTS in Exodus
Then the Lord will create a cloud of smoke by day and a glowing flame of fire by night over the entire site of Mount Zion and over its assemblies. For there will be a canopy over all the glory, and there will be a shelter for shade from heat by day and a refuge and shelter from storm and rain (Isa 4:5–6).	For the cloud of the Lord was over the tabernacle by day, and there was a fire inside the cloud by night, visible to the entire house of Israel throughout all the stages of their journey (Exod 40:38).
This is what the Lord says—who makes a way in the sea, and a path through raging water, who brings out the chariot and horse, the army and the mighty one together (they lie down, they do not rise again; they are extinguished, put out like a wick)—"Do not remember the past events; pay no attention to things of old. Look, I am about to do something new; even now it is coming. Do you not see it? Indeed, I will make a way in the wilderness, rivers in the desert (Isa 43:16–19).	The Egyptians—all Pharaoh's horses and chariots, his horsemen, and his army—chased after them and caught up with them as they camped by the sea beside Pi-hahiroth, in front of Baal-zephon (Exod 14:9).

Wake up, wake up! Arm of the Lord, clothe yourself with strength. Wake up as in days past, as in generations long ago. Wasn't it you who hacked Rahab to pieces, who pierced the sea monster? Wasn't it you who dried up the sea, the waters of the great deep, who made the sea-bed into a road for the redeemed to pass over? And the ransomed of the Lord will return and come to Zion with singing, crowned with unending joy. Joy and gladness will overtake them, and sorrow and sighing will flee (Isa 51:9–11).	With your faithful love, you will lead the people you have redeemed; you will guide them to your holy dwelling with your strength. When the peoples hear, they will shudder. . . . Terror and dread will fall on them. They will be as still as a stone because of your powerful arm until your people pass by, Lord, until the people whom you purchased pass by (Exod 15:13–14a, 16).

Cloud by day and fire by night. Passing through sea. Chariots thwarted in the sea. Passing over. These samples do not exhaust Isaiah's use of exodus allusions.[44] Claus Westermann writes that, especially in Isaiah 40–66, the exodus theme "is so conspicuous that all the other events in Israel's history recede into the background," and it creates a narrative "arc" from the exodus to the prophet's era.[45]

By alluding to the exodus, Isaiah is demonstrating the unity of the biblical metanarrative. Not only does the way God acted in the exodus provide a paradigm for how he will treat Israel subsequently, but both the first exodus and Isaiah's new exodus provide a framework for the Gospels'

[44] Bernhard Anderson lists ten texts in Isaiah 40–55 alone that employ exodus imagery: Isa 40:3–5; 41:17–20; 42:14–16; 43:1–3; 43:14–12; 48:20–21; 49:8–12; 51:9–10; 52:11–12; 55:12–13. Bernhard W. Anderson, "Exodus Typology in Second Isaiah," in *Israel's Prophetic Heritage: Essays in Honor of James Muilenburg* (Harper & Bros., 1962), 181–82.

[45] Claus Westermann, *Isaiah 40–66*, OTL (WJK, 1969), 22.

writers to convey the continuity of the biblical metanarrative in the life, death, resurrection, and ascension of Jesus Christ (cf., Mark 1:1–3; Luke 9:31). Tracing the unity of the biblical metanarrative is another key feature in evangelical biblical theology, and Old Testament allusions help us see the warp and woof of that metanarrative.

Conclusion: A Foundational Presupposition

This book presupposes something about Christian Scripture (i.e., the sixty-six canonical books of the Old and New Testaments): that (1) biblical writers respect the original context of the texts they allude to, and therefore, that (2) their use of that text will offer clarity concerning the source text. This presupposition is rooted in the unity of God's revelation in Christian Scripture orchestrated by the divine author himself.[46] This presupposition is difficult to prove wholesale, but readers can judge whether it holds in the examples given in this book and the passages readers study with the instincts offered in this book.

---

[46] This presupposition is loosely based on Bruce Waltke's "canonical process" method for studying the Psalms. He argues that individual psalms can be viewed from four "vistas": (1) the original composition, (2) the psalm's role in its subcollection (e.g., the psalms of lament in Pss 120–134), (3) the psalm's placement in the Book of Psalms, and (4) the psalm's use or relationship to the New Testament. However, in the way the psalm is used in vistas 2–4, "the original authorial intention [of a psalm] was not changed in the progressive development of the canon but deepened and clarified." Bruce K. Waltke, "A Canonical Process Approach to the Psalms," in *Tradition and Testament: Essays in Honor of Charles Lee Feinberg*, ed. John S. Feinberg (Moody, 1981), 8–9.

2

Summarizing and Situating the Three Essential Instincts

Introduction

"Excrement," contends the fictional Professor John Keating. "We're not laying pipe; we're talking about poetry." Keating, played by Robin Williams in the movie *Dead Poets Society*, thus describes the mechanical literary criticism prescribed by the fictional author, J. Evans Pritchard, in his student textbook, *Understanding Poetry*. Keating goes on to say, "Rip it out! . . . Be gone, J. Evans Pritchard, PhD. . . . This is a battle, a war, and the casualties could be your heart and soul. Armies of academics going forward measuring poetry. No! We will not have that here. . . . Now in my class, you will learn to think for yourselves again. You will learn to savor words and language."[1]

[1] *Dead Poets Society*, directed by Peter Weir (Touchstone Pictures, 1989), 22:36–24:55.

Keating's rhetorical flair is enough to give any teacher goose bumps. Oh, to inspire teenagers with such abandon! Although Keating's approach to literature is not without its critics,[2] I have heard or read enough lifelessly analytical exegesis in my life to keep Keating's critique in mind. G. K. Beale, writing about the New Testament use of the Old Testament, warns that "the task of interpretation is not merely a science but also a literary art, which defies the following of strict rules."[3]

Warnings like Beale's necessitate the following disclaimer: the method outlined in this book is not meant to be a mechanical formula like what Keating criticized in Pritchard's book. Please do not expect that inserting lexical data will spit out a vacuum-sealed conclusion on an Old Testament text's use of Scripture. I will try to do my part to walk the tightrope between turning art into science, on the one hand, and avoiding a close reading of the text, on the other. The first line of defense will be using the word *instincts* instead of the word *steps*.[4] *Step* connotes pragmatism. *Instinct* connotes subject matter that can't be mastered but must be studied.[5]

---

[2] Kevin Dettmar, "*Dead Poets Society* Is a Terrible Defense of the Humanities," *Atlantic*, February 19, 2014, https://www.theatlantic.com/education/archive/2014/02/-em-dead-poets-society-em-is-a-terrible-defense-of-the-humanities/283853/. Christian critique of *Dead Poets Society* also needs to reckon with the film's antitraditional romanticism, handled well at various points throughout Mark Eckel, *When the Lights Go Down: Movie Review as Christian Practice* (Westbow, 2014).

[3] G. K. Beale, *Handbook on the New Testament Use of the Old Testament: Exegesis and Interpretation* (Baker Academic, 2012), 41.

[4] Beale still uses the word *steps* throughout his handbook, so my distinction is simply heuristic.

[5] Some time after I wrote this chapter, Matthew Harmon and Gary Edward Schnittjer released a book that, among several important arguments, advocates for the terms "instincts" and "sensibilities" to conceptualize how to approach Scripture's use of Scripture. Matthew S. Harmon and Gary Edward Schnittjer, *How to Study the Bible's Use of the Bible: Seven Hermeneutical Choices for the Old and New Testaments* (Zondervan Academic, 2024), 83.

Three Essential Instincts

Sometimes it all starts with a hunch. Sometimes, the more we read the Old Testament, the more its idiom gets into our imagination, so we notice something in one passage reminiscent of another passage. Sometimes we hear about a potential connection between passages in a sermon or read about it in a commentary. Something in a biblical passage piques the memory of another biblical passage. Ziva Ben-Porat calls the *something* that triggers the connection a "marker." The allusion marker might be a word, a phrase, a personal name, or a place-name.[6] Hosea 9:9 marks its allusion to an event in Judges with the brief phrase "as in the days of Gibeah." Micah 7:19 marks its allusion to Exodus 15 with one word: "depths."[7] It all starts with noticing a similarity between biblical texts—how pedestrian! This is an exciting aspect of serious Bible study for at least two reasons. First, the possibilities are vastly untapped. Scripture's multifaceted, inexhaustible depth means that there are possible scriptural allusions no one has noticed or articulated yet.[8] Others have been noticed, but not yet deeply engaged.[9] Unmined treasure exists in the pages of the

---

[6] Ziva Ben-Porat, "The Poetics of Literary Allusion," *PTL: A Journal for Descriptive Poetics and Theory of Literature* 1 (1976): 110.

[7] See chapter 1 for a brief overview of this allusion.

[8] For a fascinating example of a New Testament allusion to the Old Testament that went "widely ignored" and the possibility of which was "not even raised," see Dane C. Ortlund, "'And Their Eyes Were Opened, and They Knew': An Inter-Canonical Note on Luke 24:31," *JETS* 53, no. 4 (2010): 721.

[9] *Mention* without *sustained engagement* led to the concept for my doctoral dissertation on the use of Judges in Psalms. My mentor and friend Paul House once wrote, "The multiple appearances of judges-era . . . references later in the canon indicate that these episodes may need more treatment in Biblical Theology than they have received in the past." Paul R. House, "Examining the Narratives of Old Testament Narrative: An Exploration in Biblical Theology," *WTJ* 67 (2005): 237–38. That statement became like a rock in my shoe that led me to Psalms literature—where allusions to the exodus dominate scholarship. I noticed that commentaries mentioned allusions to Judges in Psalms 68, 83, and 106, but without sustained analysis. For what it's worth, in the original quotation, House

Bible, and especially the Old Testament.[10] Second, the more one learns the whole Bible, the more likely one is to notice markers intended by biblical authors.

But is the marker intended by the author, or merely a hunch? The case must be investigated. I have read every legal and detective procedural novel written by Michael Connelly. So, the following analogy is built not on legitimate legal training but on countless hours of fictional training. When exploring—or mounting—an evidential case, I think of Connelly's fictional lawyerly protagonist, Mickey Haller: the Lincoln Lawyer. Once, while defending an accused murderer, Mickey praised the opposing lawyer's case because the prosecution had three things going for them: hard evidence, circumstantial evidence, and a resultant "cumulative" narrative.[11] We want the same three things when exploring a potential allusion.

1) Hard Evidence: Terms

Mickey taught me that DNA makes a jury's job easy.[12] It's hard evidence. Perhaps the hardest evidence one can provide. When exploring a potential allusion, *shared terms* are the hardest evidence one can provide. Hebrew vocabulary is the DNA in an Old Testament allusion case. Jeffery

---

also mentions the wilderness wandering era. Perhaps you, reader, will write the definitive study on the use of Numbers in later Old Testament books.

[10] The scholarly field of New Testament use of the Old Testament is more developed than the Old Testament use of the Old Testament. When I reread this paragraph, I realized it might sound to some like a denial of the Protestant doctrine of the clarity of Scripture. Recall the discussion in chapter 1 about Judges 19, and how the *general message* of the narrative can be grasped even without grasping the *particular nuances* of an allusion. So, I am not implying that texts remain completely misunderstood until unmined allusions are engaged, but I am suggesting that there are nuances in many texts that may be heretofore unnoticed or underappreciated.

[11] Michael Connelly, *The Fifth Witness* (Little, Brown, 2011), 402.

[12] Connelly, 268.

Leonard calls shared terms "the surest guide to establishing allusions."[13] No matter how similar two texts seem, without shared terms, it is difficult to establish a connection with any certainty.[14] Chapter 3 will explore the kinds and combinations of terms that constitute a "secure" case.[15]

2) Circumstantial Evidence: Themes

Still, you will need more than DNA to beat Mickey Haller: "That doesn't mean there isn't an explanation for it. I'll handle the DNA."[16] Circumstantial evidence either clinches or explains away DNA evidence. You'll need more than shared terms to establish an allusion. As chapter 3 will explore, many factors other than an allusion can result in shared terms. More is needed. The circumstantial evidence in an allusion case is what Richard Schultz calls "contextual awareness."[17] Basically, if the contexts of the alluding and source texts have themes in common, it raises the probability that the alluding author had the source text in mind.

3) Cumulative Narrative: Thesis

"A trial often comes down to who is a better storyteller, the prosecution or the defense," notes Mickey Haller in Michael Connelly's 2005 novel *The Law of Evidence*. "There is evidence, of course, but physical evidence

---

[13] Jeffery M. Leonard, "Identifying Subtle Allusions: The Promise of Narrative Tracking," *Subtle Citation, Allusion, and Translation in the Hebrew Bible* (Equinox, 2017), 95.

[14] For a notable exception, built on a shared "uncommon" metaphor (i.e., washing away sin) rather than shared terms, see Lesley DiFransico, "Identifying Inner-Biblical Allusion through Metaphor: Washing Away Sin in Psalm 51," VT 65, no. 4 (2015): 542–57.

[15] Leonard, "Identifying Subtle Allusions," 95.

[16] Connelly, *Fifth Witness*, 268.

[17] Richard L. Schultz, *The Search for Quotation: Verbal Parallels in the Prophets*, JSOTSS 180 (Sheffield Academic, 1999), 224–25.

is at first interpreted for the jury by the storyteller."[18] Evidence, both the hard and circumstantial type, needs to make sense within a larger, persuasive story. This is where a lawyer's *rhetorical* flair comes into play (in my extensive fictional courtroom experience). Jewish scholar Michael Fishbane explains that when an Old Testament text uses another text, it does so for "rhetorical effect" and with a "rhetorical goal."[19] If so, then the rhetorical effect of an alluding text should become clearer once the allusion is understood. Grasping the allusion should help the interpreter grasp the text's overall *thesis*.[20] This third instinct, then, involves investigating the rhetorical goal of the alluding text to determine if and how the source text enhances the rhetorical force of the alluding text.

Situating the Instincts

As instincts grow surrounding the terms, themes, and theses involved in Old Testament allusions, facility in identifying and engaging allusions will also grow. The instincts might make a bit more sense after a *brief* survey of the Old Testament use of the Old Testament field. Michael Fishbane is often credited with initiating scholarly inquiry into the topic.[21] One of the most important critiques of his work was that his

---

[18] Michael Connelly, *The Law of Innocence* (Little, Brown, 2020), 190.

[19] Michael Fishbane, *Biblical Interpretation in Ancient Israel*, repr. ed. (Clarendon, 1989), 200, 417.

[20] In NT use of the OT studies, Richard Hays talks about something like this in the criterion of *satisfaction*. There should be an exegetically satisfying effect to grasping an allusion if the allusion is indeed part of the alluding text's rhetorical goal. Richard B. Hays, *Echoes of Scripture in the Letters of Paul* (Yale University Press, 1989), 32.

[21] James Kugel asked, "Why has it taken until now for a full-length survey of 'inner-biblical interpretation'—that is, the phenomenon of biblical texts that seem to interpret, rework, or otherwise elaborate upon other biblical texts—to see the light of day?" James Kugel, "The Bible's Earliest Interpreters," *Prooftexts* 7, no. 3 (1987): 269. Leonard explains that while

method did not provide a way to arbitrate proposed allusions that are not self-evident.[22] But he still sounded the starting gun, sending the field on a quest for firm identification criteria.

The first and most obvious criterion that emerged was to use *terms* to identify allusions.[23] However, shared terms can be explained in many ways other than an allusion. For example, two texts might be using "formulaic, idiomatic or proverbial language."[24] Schultz's solution was to encourage interpreters to look for evidence that the alluding author possessed "contextual awareness" of the source text, for example, by using images from the source text's context.[25] This trend is reflected in the *themes* instinct in this study.

Ever since Fishbane, though, there was a thread at which scholars seemed to tug but not pull with full force: rhetoric. I mentioned previously that Fishbane saw Scripture's use of Scripture as possessing both "rhetorical effect" and a "rhetorical goal."[26] The issue of rhetoric never seemed to be (in my opinion) consistently explored in a way that could be reproduced by others in the field of inner-biblical allusion studies (because reproducible methods for rhetorical analysis certainly did exist,

---

interpreters were well aware of the phenomenon of inner-biblical reuse, as critical Old Testament study grew, "it was more than a century before the first systematic treatment of inner-biblical exegesis emerged in the form of Michael Fishbane's *Biblical Interpretation in Ancient Israel.*" Jeffery Leonard, "Inner-Biblical Interpretation and Intertextuality," in *Literary Approaches to the Bible*, ed. Douglas Mangum and Douglas Estes, Lexham Methods Series (Lexham, 2018), 60.

[22] Kugel, "Earliest Interpreters," 274–77.

[23] For example, James Nogalski laid out a methodology in 1996 that relied mostly on terms. James D. Nogalski, "Intertextuality in the Twelve," in *Forming Prophetic Literature: Essays on Isaiah and the Twelve in Honor of John D. W. Watts*, JSOTSS 235 (Sheffield Academic, 1996), 109–10.

[24] Schultz, *Search for Quotation*, 224–25.

[25] Schultz, 224–25.

[26] Fishbane, *Biblical Interpretation in Ancient Israel*, 200, 417.

but in the separate field of rhetorical criticism).[27] This book tries to offer something substantial yet reproducible in the rhetorical area we will call the *thesis*, or the alluding text's persuasive reason for using the source text. The use of rhetorical criticism should help both analyze and confirm the nature of the allusion, because if the allusion is legitimate, it will enhance the interpreter's grasp of the rhetorical goals of the alluding text itself.

All that to say, the three instincts employed in this book represent two best practices (terms and themes) in the field and one I think could help a lot more than it has (theses). But first, two technical matters need to be addressed.

Direction and Availability

My wife Jackie and I are embroiled in an irresolvable debate. Through casual research, I found that the '90s sitcom *Seinfeld* coined the phrase "double-dipping" (George, of course, double-dipping at a funeral).[28] That episode aired in 1993. Jackie claims, however, that her father was enforcing double-dipping restrictions—and using the phrase to do so—before 1993. Can you see why it's irresolvable? If Jackie could somehow accurately date her double-dipping memories to, let's say 1991, the matter could be resolved. Something like this occurs in biblical studies when

---

[27] For example, Schultz encourages analyzing the use of Scripture in the OT as a "rhetorical device," but then applies this step differently with each text he analyzes. Schultz, *Search for Quotation*, 233, 255–307. Recent studies commendably devote more attention to this aspect of allusions, but again, not necessarily in ways that are consistent and reproducible. For example, see the excellent study by Brooke G. Lester, *Daniel Evokes Isaiah: Allusive Characterization of Foreign Rule in the Hebrew-Aramaic Book of Daniel*, LHBOTS 606 (Bloomsbury, 2015).

[28] Max Gross, "Seinfeld's 25 Greatest Contributions to the English Language," *New York Post*, July 1, 2014, https://nypost.com/2014/07/01/the-25-best-seinfeld-isms/. For what it's worth, when I typed *phrases coined by* into a Google search bar, the top suggestion for finishing my search phrase was *Shakespeare*. The second was *Seinfeld*. Do with that information what you'd like.

the claim is made of an Old Testament allusion: who borrowed from whom (direction of dependence), and even who *could have* borrowed from whom (availability)?

There are two general ways to answer the questions of direction of dependence (i.e., which text borrowed from the other) and availability (i.e., whether a source text was available to the potential alluding text). The first general approach is known as **synchronic**, which uses the two texts in question to deduce who borrowed from whom. Synchronic approaches to biblical studies prioritize literary issues (i.e., the texts themselves). The second approach is known as **diachronic**, which uses standard critical methods to determine the historical background of the texts involved. Diachronic approaches to biblical studies prioritize historical questions (i.e., behind the texts involved). On some level, both need to be kept in mind, though this book will tend toward synchronic emphases while seeking not to ignore diachronic issues.[29]

1) Who Borrowed from Whom? (The Synchronic Question)

Two questions can help interpreters determine who borrowed from whom. First, *Which text can stand alone without reference to the other?*[30] The source text stands on its own. Leonard offers the following example. Genesis 12:10–20 tells the story of Abram's trip to Egypt in a way reminiscent of Israel's collective journey to and out of Egypt: famine, relocation, danger, plagues, and acquiring wealth on the way out. Which story can stand alone without reference to the other, the exodus or Abram's journey? Leonard explains, "It is nearly impossible . . .

[29] As a matter of emphasis, this facilitates spending most of our time in this book on the words and theology of the biblical text rather than on dating and historical reconstruction.

[30] See Cynthia Edenburg, "How (Not) to Murder a King: Variations on a Theme in 1 Sam 24; 26," *SJOT* 12 (1998): 73–74; Jeffery M. Leonard, "Identifying Inner-Biblical Allusions: Psalm 78 as a Test Case," *JBL* 127, no. 2 (2008), 260–62.

to understand how an isolated pericope in Abram's story could have given birth to the great complex of traditions that make up the exodus story."[31] So Genesis 12 is probably patterned after Exodus.[32] The same is true of the example from Judges 19 that opens chapter 1 in this book. The scathing critique of Gibeah presupposes Sodom and Gomorrah in Genesis 19, not the other way around. Chapter 1 also mentions Mic 7:19 alluding to Exodus 15. Since the former is a metaphorical play on the latter, the metaphor relies on the literal event rather than the other way around.

Second, *Which text is more likely to be a borrower?*[33] I often see the same toy in the hands of my oldest and youngest sons at different times. It so happens that my youngest likes to help himself to his older brother's toys. So, if there is a dispute, I can usually tell who borrowed from whom! Something like this often helps with determining the direction of dependence in an Old Testament allusion. For example, Pss 135:15–18 and 115:4–8 are identical.[34] Who borrowed from whom? Since, as Leslie Allen notes, Psalm 135 is "a conglomeration of snatches from other parts

---

[31] Leonard, "Identifying Inner-Biblical Allusions," 260.

[32] Though Leonard does not assume Mosaic authorship, as I do (and regardless of whether Moses wrote Genesis 12 or Exodus 7–12 first), Moses probably experienced the exodus from Egypt before he wrote about Abram's journey to and from Egypt. Thus, he was able to narrate Gen 12:10–20 in a way that would feel familiar, resonant, and encouraging to the Israelites who had recently left Egypt. John H. Sailhamer says, "By shaping the account of Abraham's sojourn in Egypt to parallel the events of the Exodus, the author permits the reader to see the implications of God's past deeds with his chosen people." Sailhamer, *The Pentateuch as Narrative: A Biblical-Theological Commentary* (Zondervan, 1995), 142.

[33] Leonard, "Identifying Inner-Biblical Allusions," 262–63. I have given two of the more accessible criteria for determining the direction of dependence here. For a more advanced list, see Leonard, "Inner-Biblical Interpretation and Intertextuality," 56–58.

[34] The length of shared language qualifies this as a quotation rather than an allusion, a distinction explained in chapter 1.

of the OT,"[35] it is far more likely that 135 borrows from 115 than the other way around. In fact, Psalm 135 is one of five psalms known as historical psalms (Pss 78; 105–106; 135–136) that are known for rehearsing several episodes in Old Testament history to convince those singing each psalm to remember, repent, praise, etc. Therefore, when words and themes are shared by one of those psalms and another Old Testament text, chances are the historical psalms are the borrowers.

Sometimes the direction may not be able to be determined. Back to my children and their toys. There is also the possibility that both of my sons have snatched—nay, borrowed—an item from my daughter (the middle child). This possibility needs to be kept in mind when two texts have terms and themes in common. Sometimes, rather than one borrowing from the other, they both borrow from another source. The other source might be a common phrase like the liturgical one shared by Ps 106:1 and Ps 107:1, "Give thanks to the Lord, for he is good; his faithful love endures forever." Or sometimes it might be impossible to tell with certainty whether one borrowed from the other or both borrowed from a third source. Isaiah 2:2–4 and Mic 4:1–4 are notorious in this regard. No one doubts that the texts are related, but as Brevard Childs writes, "Evidence for the priority of either Isaiah or Micah is inconclusive. It is possible that the passage predated both prophets and was accommodated by each collection in a slightly different form."[36]

2) What Was Available to the Alluding Author? (The Diachronic Question)

In Stephen King's *11.22.63*, Jake Epping travels from the present day to 1960 to hatch a three-year strategy to prevent President Kennedy's assassination in 1963. As an English teacher and lover of books, Jake

[35] Leslie C. Allen, *Psalms 101–150*, 2nd ed., WBC 21 (Zondervan, 2018), 224.

[36] Brevard S. Childs, *Isaiah: A Commentary*, OTL (WJK, 2001), 28.

must be careful not to allude to novels not yet written. Why? Because one does not allude to cultural artifacts not yet created! The only time I can think it appropriate to allude to the future rather than the past is in the rare case of time travel. As Richard Schultz notes, the Old Testament use of the Old Testament is "a historical phenomenon" with "a unique chronological dimension."[37] If there seems to be an allusion in one text to another, it matters whether the potential source text was even written and available at the time of the alluding text's writing. If it seems like a Davidic psalm is alluding to Malachi, for example, it probably is an illusion rather than an allusion. One can avoid this question when studying the New Testament use of the Old Testament, because even the most critical scholars agree that the Old Testament is, well, older than the new one.

Anyone who has taken a class or read a commentary introduction in the Old Testament knows how contentious *dating* Old Testament texts can be. I cannot think of one Old Testament book about which the date is an agreeable matter among scholars. That does not mean, however, that the issue does not need to be addressed while identifying and analyzing Old Testament allusions. It just means that conclusions may need to be "tentative" and held humbly.[38]

In broad terms, Figure 1 demonstrates the *potential* and *reasonable* availability of each biblical book to subsequent biblical writers. If biblical book A stands to the left of biblical book B on the timeline, it would not be unreasonable to build a case for book B to have alluded to book A. Because debates about dating the final form of biblical books often fall along so-called critical and conservative lines—and you may have noticed that I am the latter—readers might want to consult scholarship more in line with their convictions. To aim for as much breadth as possible within a conservative confessional standpoint, Figure 1 represents the dating

---

[37] Schultz, *Search for Quotation*, 227.
[38] Schultz, 231.

Figure 1: Timeline of OT Book Availability

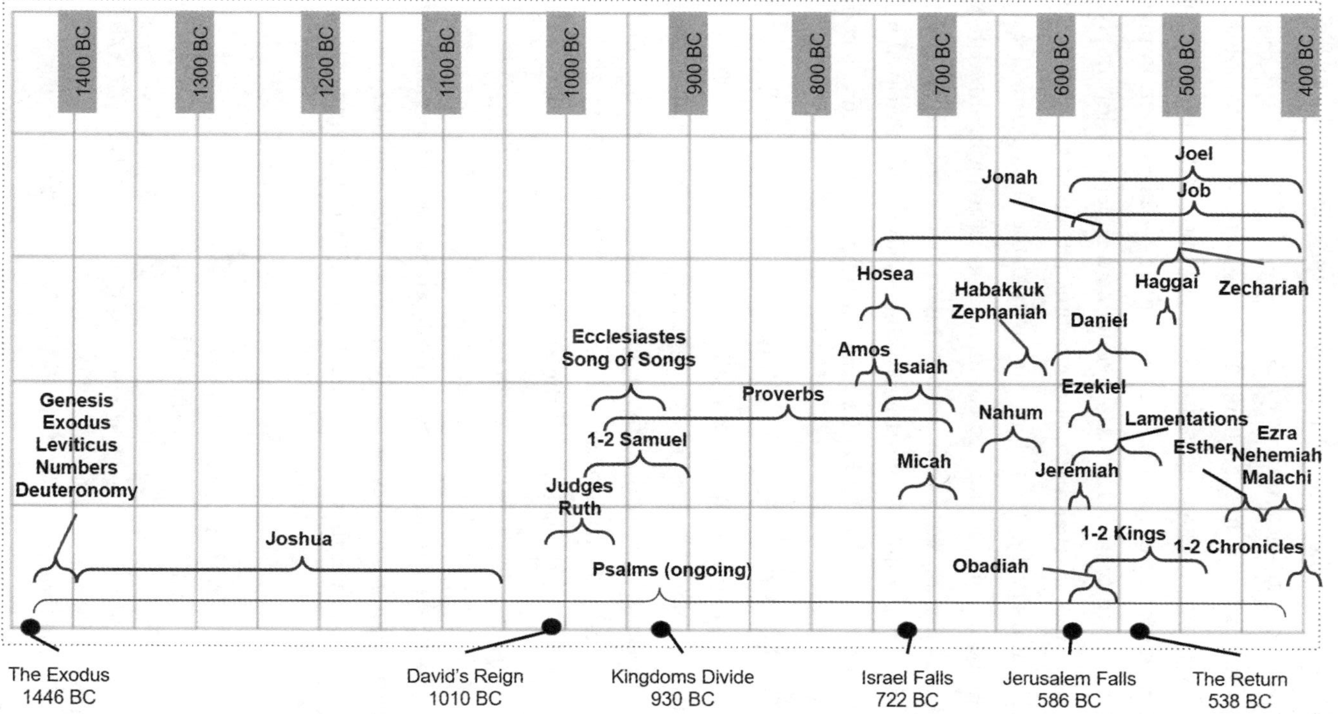

conclusions of the thirty-four scholars responsible for the Old Testament introductory articles in the *ESV Study Bible*.[39]

One caveat is needed here. Many, or some would say most, biblical books underwent a compositional *process*. The Psalter presents the clearest example. Seventy-three psalms contain superscription implying that David wrote them. One psalm contains a superscription implying that Moses wrote it (Psalm 90). Some psalms reflect on the exile (Psalm 137) and return (Psalm 107). This means that the **final form** of the Psalms took about a millennium to complete. Therefore, a finalized Psalter was not available to, say, Isaiah. But that doesn't mean Isaiah could not have alluded to a psalm. So, whether he alludes to this or that psalm depends not on the date for the book's final form but the date for its component poems and songs.

Psalm 68 (a Davidic psalm) offers another example. The psalm possesses a quotation and several allusions to Judges 5 (Deborah's Song). Although figure 1 does not demonstrate this issue, many conservative scholars date the final form of Judges to sometime after 722 BC. In Judg 18:30 the narrator says a worship site existed "until the time of the exile from the land," and the earliest self-evident exile, or "captivity" (ESV), is the northern kingdom's exile and fall of Samaria in 722 BC.[40] How then could David, reigning from 1010 to 970 BC, have access to Judges 5? According to the critical scholarship of Susan Niditch, for example, Judges 5 "may be one of the most ancient works of the Hebrew Bible."[41] Although scholars like Niditch would almost certainly deny

---

[39] Lane T. Dennis, ed., *ESV Study Bible* (Crossway, 2008).

[40] For example, Ian M. Duguid, "Introduction to Judges," *CSB Study Bible* (Holman Bible, 2017), 360. For a plausible argument for a final form of Judges during the lifetime of David, however, see E. J. Young, *An Introduction to the Old Testament* (Eerdmans, 1989), 169–70.

[41] Susan Niditch, *Judges*, OTL (WJK, 2008), 76. Substantial Mosaic authorship of the Pentateuch would of course provide plenty of texts older than Deborah.

Davidic authorship of Psalm 68,[42] they would probably grant that the Song of Deborah could have been available in a form other than the final form in the early tenth century BC when King David reigned. So do not fret if figure 1, or the dating scheme of your favorite commentary or OT introduction, makes it seem like a particular allusion is not possible. Sometimes an alluding text might refer to a tradition or early form of what would later be crystallized in the final form of a biblical book.[43]

These two approaches—synchronic and diachronic—should both be kept in mind when investigating a potential allusion. Due to the intricacies of both approaches, sometimes certainty will not be possible. But if Christian tradition teaches us anything about using Scripture to interpret Scripture (the analogy of faith), the church does not need a demonstrable allusive relationship between texts for their comparison to be exegetically and spiritually fruitful. Best-case scenario: a source text proves integral to the alluding text's argument and amplifies the alluding text's meaning. Worst-case scenario: two texts in dialogue cause the interpreter to think freshly about the interconnected, mutually interpreting beauty of God's Word.[44]

---

[42] For one of the most vigorous recent defenses of the reliability of Davidic superscriptions, see the introduction to James M. Hamilton Jr., *Psalms*, vol. 1, EBTC (Lexham, 2021).

[43] One of my (then) students, Andrew Klein, pointed out an excellent example in Hos 9:9's use of the "days of Gibeah." This almost certainly refers to Judges 19's infamous Gibeah incident (see "Introduction" in chapter 1). If indeed Judges was not a completed book until after 722 BC, and Hosea ministered before the fall of Samaria in 722 BC, then Hos 9:9 would be referring to something like a tradition, memory, or earlier written form of Judges 19 rather than the chapter as it is currently situated in Judges.

[44] For example, Beth LaNeel Tanner reads two of the OT's darkest texts alongside one another (Judges 19; Psalm 88), not because she claims that there is an intentional allusion or quotation at play, but because the pairing moves the interpreter to consider overlapping experiences of horror and suffering. Beth LaNeel Tanner, *The Book of Psalms Through the Lens of Intertextuality*, StBibLit 26 (Peter Lang, 2001), 53, 159–80.

In the classic 1990s comedy film *City Slickers*, one ice cream mogul asks another what the perfect ice cream pairing would be with their meal of franks and beans. "Cherry vanilla?" His counterpart answers, "No. If it was Chinese food—right on the money. But this? Toasted almond." Amazed, the incorrect guesser declares, "Barry can pick out the exact right flavor of ice cream to follow any meal."[45] Maybe the investigation of a potential allusion will reveal a genuine allusion—the perfect (i.e., author-intended) pairing like Barry's toasted almond. But if the allusion is not genuine, pairing two texts together for reflection will still taste good—like cherry vanilla.

Conclusion

As a former naval doctor, my father—the original Dr. Swale—received some of the same training that his pilot patients underwent. He needed to know the instincts *and* physical faculties involved in his patients' responsibilities so he could assess when his patients were fit for duty. So, when called upon to assess whether a helicopter pilot was ready to fly again, my dad knew experientially what the patient needed to be able to do. He couldn't just *hear* a briefing about the physical demands and instincts needed for their duties, he needed to be *immersed* in the complexities of those demands and instincts. This chapter briefed you on the instincts (terms, themes, theses) and issues (synchronic and diachronic) needed to identify and analyze Old Testament allusions. It's time to move beyond a briefing and immerse you in the interpretive complexities that each of the three instincts entails. Chapter 3 will deal with terms, chapter 4 with themes, and chapter 5 with rhetorical theses.

---

[45] *City Slickers*, directed by Ron Underwood (Castle Rock Entertainment, 1991), 1:04:38–1:06:07.

3

Instinct 1: Terms—Anchor the Allusion

Introduction

"Sometimes I wonder if you believe you've got the market on grief cornered." A fictitious cowboy thought he could end this lovers' quarrel by replying, "I've never said that." Nice try. "Not in so many words you haven't," his lover replied. The cowboy's answer was brilliant but got him nowhere in the spat: "There's no other way to say a thing but in words."[1]

In love and war, the cowboy is wrong. But when it comes to Old Testament allusions, he's correct: there's no other way to allude to a text than words. Because terms will always be the "surest guide" to identifying Old Testament allusions,[2] shared words provide an anchor for the allusion identification process. The next two sections lay out three *don'ts* and

[1] Larry Watson, *As Good as Gone: A Novel* (Algonquin, 2016), 366.

[2] Jeffery M. Leonard, "Identifying Subtle Allusions: The Promise of Narrative Tracking," in *Subtle Citation, Allusion, and Translation in the Hebrew Bible*, ed. Ziony Zevit (Equinox, 2017), 95.

three *dos* for anchoring an allusion in the terms shared by an alluding text and a source text.

How Not to Anchor an Allusion with Terms

1) Not in English Terms

While the Old Testament was written in Hebrew, with a few brief sections in Aramaic,[3] most people reading this book will first encounter or sense a potential allusion in an English translation. Allusions cannot be verified in English, though, for two reasons. First, the same word or concept in English might represent different Hebrew words. For example, the word *love* in an English translation of the Old Testament might represent the Hebrew nouns *'ahăḇâ* or *ḥeseḏ*. The former is a general word for *love*, while the latter is translated into English in a variety of ways that sometimes contain the English word *love*: "faithful love" (CSB), "steadfast love" (ESV), "great love" (NIV), etc. We would not be able to verify an allusion based on the English word *love* if the texts included these two terms without checking to see if they are the same Hebrew word.

Consider Gen 3:15. This beautiful passage, often called the *protoevangelion* for its initiation of messianic hope, contains several themes that recur throughout the rest of the Old Testament. While there are Old Testament passages that allude to Gen 3:15,[4] it is possible to see allusions to Gen 3:15 where they cannot be firmly verified. In some of these cases, English terms can be misleading, like in Ps 68:23. A few interpreters mention the word *foot* in Ps 68:23 as indicative of an allusion to the

[3] Ezra 4:8–6:18; 7:12–26; Jer 10:11; Dan 2:4b–7:28. A. Jeffery, "Hebrew Language," *The Interpreter's Dictionary of the Bible*, vol. 2 (Abingdon, 1985), 553.

[4] Schnittjer lists three: Isa 25:10b–12; 65:25; and Mic 7:17, though these allusions also involve Gen 3:14. Gary Edward Schnittjer, *Old Testament Use of Old Testament: A Book-by-Book Guide* (Zondervan, 2021), 1.

serpent's strike in Gen 3:15.[5] Psalm 68:23, however, uses the primary Hebrew word for *foot* (*regel*), whereas Gen 3:15 uses a word for the *heel* (*ʿāqēḇ*). There may be an allusion *afoot*, but Hebrew words in common would be the place to start rather than English ones.

Second, English terms might also lead a Bible reader in the opposite direction: not realizing two texts use the same Hebrew word(s). This phenomenon works against helping readers notice allusions. For example, when Samson insists his parents arrange a marriage with a Philistine woman, he says, "She's the right one for me" (Judg 14:3b). The Hebrew words in Samson's idiom literally read, "She is right (*yāšar*) in my eyes (*ʿayin*)." The wording, most notably *yāšar* and *ʿayin*, "links" Samson's actions to the wider problem of Israel doing what is right (*yāšar*) in their own eyes (*ʿayin*) (Judg 17:6; 21:25 ESV).[6] Judges 14:4, then, implies that Samson embodies the same collective spiritual autonomy that leads to the covenantal dysfunction for Israel in the book of Judges. Together, the three texts using *yāšar* and *ʿayin* in Judges (14:4; 17:6; 21:25) allude to Deut 12:8 where Moses warns, "You are not to do as we are doing here today; everyone is doing what seems right (*yāšar*) in his own sight (*ʿayin*)." This allusion adds texture to the indictment in Judg 14:4; 17:6; and 21:25: not only are Samson and Israel defining their own morality,

---

[5] This example does not do justice to the fullness of these interpreters' sophisticated arguments, but someone reading their work may conclude that the word *foot* suggests an allusion to Gen 3:15. In the works cited here, these scholars do not mention that the foot imagery employs different Hebrew words. Trevor Laurence writes, "Psalm 68 announces that God will strike the hairy crown of his enemies' heads (v. 21) and have his people strike their feet in the foes' blood (v. 23), weaving together imagery of the *protoevangelion* [and Deut 32:42]." Trevor Laurence, "Serpent Seed and Son of God: The Enemy and the Imprecator in the Psalms of Vengeance," *CTR* 17, no. 2 (Spr 2020): 108. See also James M. Hamilton Jr., "The Skull-Crushing Seed of the Woman: Inner-Biblical Interpretation of Genesis 3:15," *SBJT* 10, no. 2 (2006): 37.

[6] Mark Boda and Mary Conway, *Judges*, ZECOT (Zondervan, 2022), 616.

but they are also failing to heed God's Word in Deut 12:8.[7] In English alone, the allusion in Judg 14:3 would be difficult to detect.

There's no way around an awkward conclusion: pinning down Old Testament allusions means dabbling in Hebrew. Do not fear. You do not need to take a Hebrew class (though they are more accessible nowadays than ever). There are several ways to investigate the Hebrew word represented in an English translation. For a price, Bible software like Logos or Accordance provides Bible students with easy ways to identify Hebrew words and whether potential alluding and source texts use the same terms. The interlinear functions of free websites like Blue Letter Bible and STEP Bible also enable Bible students to find this information. We live in a time where through the right software or website, the Hebrew word behind an English Bible translation is one click away.

2) Not in Common Terms

Ed Sheeran's 2023 defense against a plagiarism lawsuit—alleging that he stole a tune from the late Marvin Gaye's "Let's Get It On"—hinged on *commonness*.[8] The lawsuit alleged that the "melodic, harmonic, and rhythmic" elements in "Thinking Out Loud" were "strikingly similar" to Gaye's song.[9] By playing several well-known songs for the jury that also sound *similar* to the songs in question, Sheeran was able to successfully defend

---

[7] Jillian Ross states poignantly, "The allusion to Deut 12 contributes to Judges' overall theme, a people heeds not Scripture." Jillian L. Ross, *A People Heeds Not Scripture: Allusion in Judges* (Pickwick, 2023), 213.

[8] Larisha Paul, "Ed Sheeran Plays Van Morrison Song as Proof He Didn't Steal from Marvin Gaye in Copyright Trial," *Rolling Stone*, May 1, 2023, https://www.rollingstone.com/music/music-news/ed-sheeran-references-van-morrison-copyright-trial-1234727230/.

[9] Daniel Kreps, "Ed Sheeran Wins 'Thinking Out Loud' Copyright Trial," *Rolling Stone*, September 25, 2023, https://www.rollingstone.com/music/music-news/ed-sheeran-not-liable-thinking-out-loud-trial-1234724464/.

himself against the allegations. *Commonness* disproved *borrowing*. This is also the case in Old Testament allusions. If the shared terms between two texts are common in the Old Testament, it is difficult to say whether the author used the word to allude to another text or simply because that was a common word for the concept at hand. For example, Gen 3:15 uses the word *head*. The main Hebrew word for *head* (*rōʾš*) occurs 604 times in the Old Testament. Since the word occurs so often in the Old Testament, subsequent uses of *rōʾš* do not mean a text alludes to Gen 3:15. It also doesn't mean the text *isn't* alluding to Gen 3:15, but there would need to be additional terms shared between the two texts. We will see how common Hebrew words can be part of a cumulative case for a proposed allusion, but they should not be the only evidence.

3) Not in "Stock" Phrases

I am going to double-dip here and remind the reader of the double-dipping debate outlined in chapter 2. My wife's contention is difficult to refute because the phrase has become ubiquitous. Even if I am right about the phrase's *Seinfeld* origin, the commonness of the phrase means that most people who use the phrase today are not intentionally alluding to George Costanza's predicament. Likewise, there are words and phrases that might not be especially common but exist in the Old Testament as what Benjamin Sommer calls "stock vocabulary."[10] Double-dipping is stock vocabulary nowadays. James Nogalski uses the two-word Hebrew phrase "this is the Lord's declaration (*nᵊʾum*)" (e.g., Amos 9:13) as an example in the Old Testament. It might seem like this phrase builds a strong case for an allusion, but it occurs over 250 times in the Old Testament.[11]

[10] Benjamin D. Sommer, *A Prophet Reads Scripture: Allusions in Isaiah 40–66* (Stanford University Press, 1998), 68–71.

[11] James D. Nogalski, "Intertextuality in the Twelve," in *Forming Prophetic Literature: Essays on Isaiah and the Twelve in Honor of John D. W. Watts*, JSOTSS 235 (Sheffield Academic, 1996), 109n19.

It is a stock phrase in prophetic literature and therefore would not make a strong anchor for an allusion. Or consider the death idiom "rest with . . . ancestors" (e.g., Gen 47:30). Two texts may share this phrase, but because it occurs in some forty Old Testament passages, it is a stock idiom that can't carry the load of verifying an allusion. Like common terms, it can be a part of a cumulative case but cannot stand alone. Finally, think about the phrase "land flowing with milk and honey" in Jer 32:22. The four Hebrew words that make up the English phrase "land flowing with milk and honey" occur in the same order in Exod 3:8. Often, four Hebrew words in a row are "pinch me; I'm dreamin'" time for verifying an allusion.[12] But because the same phrase occurs verbatim in fifteen total Old Testament texts as a stock description of the fertile Promised Land,[13] it probably does not indicate an allusion by Jeremiah to any single text.

How to Anchor an Allusion with Terms

1) Yes, in Rare Terms

Because J. K. Rowling created the word "quidditch" for the Harry Potter series, someone using the word today is probably alluding to her books or the films adapted from them. Or *dinglehopper*: Disney's *The Little Mermaid* may not have made up this word, but the film popularized it. Because of the word's rarity otherwise, someone using the word is probably alluding to the film. Likewise, as Jeffery Leonard points out, in Old Testament allusions, "Shared language that is rare or distinctive suggests a stronger connection than does language that

[12] An allusion to a Vince Vaughn line in *The Dilemma*, directed by Ron Howard (Universal Pictures, 2011).

[13] The phrase connotes good pasturelands leading to productive dairy farming, and sufficient *flora* for bees to produce honey. The phrase describes both the meeting of needs (milk) and luxuries (honey).

is widely used."[14] The original language resources mentioned earlier in this chapter (Logos, Accordance, Blue Letter Bible, etc.) allow students to determine the frequency of a word in the Hebrew Old Testament, so this is not as difficult as it sounds.

For example, Hos 12:3 says that Jacob "wrestled with God." The word for "wrestled" (*śārâ*), only occurs twice in the Old Testament. Genesis 32:28 contains the other use of *śārâ*, so the likelihood that Hosea 12 alludes to Genesis 32 is very high. Or consider Ps 29:10a: "The LORD sits enthroned over the flood." "Flood," *mabûl* in Hebrew, occurs thirteen times in the Old Testament. This is not as clear as a word only occurring twice, but surveying the thirteen uses reveals that twelve of the occurrences are in one biblical story: Noah and the flood.[15] The likelihood is high, then, that Psalm 29 alludes to Genesis 6–9's flood narrative. Uncommon proper nouns can help anchor an allusion also. Psalm 83:11 mentions a nasty fellow named Zebah (Hebrew, *zeḇaḥ*). This word occurs twelve times in the Old Testament: eleven times in Judges 8, and once in Psalm 83. The likelihood is high, then, that Psalm 83 alludes to Judges 8.

2) Yes, in Uncommon (Non-Stock) Phrases

The next two ways to anchor an allusion are more easily accomplished using Bible study tools like the ones mentioned in the previous section (Logos, Accordance, Blue Letter Bible, etc.). These tools enable searches that track down the Hebrew phrases and word clusters that can anchor an allusion.[16] Using uncommon phrases to anchor an allusion might

---

[14] Jeffery M. Leonard, "Identifying Inner-Biblical Allusions: Psalm 78 as a Test Case," *JBL* 127, no. 2 (2008), 251.

[15] Schnittjer, *Old Testament Use*, 540.

[16] For a free example, click on the Strong's Number for a word in Blue Letter Bible's Interlinear function. Midway down the resultant page, there is a search function called "Word/Phrase/Strong's Search." Strong's Numbers for multiple original language words can be entered into the search box to find single verses

make more sense in modern culture because cinematic allusions usually make use of unique phrases rather than rare words. "You broke my heart" is a stock phrase in American culture, but "I knew it was you, Fredo. You broke my heart" evokes one iconic movie.[17] "You complete me" alludes to one very specific romantic film (as does, "Show me the money!").[18] Because phrases are a combination of terms, they are one of the best kinds of anchors for Old Testament allusions.[19] The terms themselves may not be rare, but putting them next to one another often is. For example, the word *this* (Hebrew, *zê*) occurs 322 times in the Old Testament, and the word *Sinai* (Hebrew, *sînay*) occurs thirty-five times. But *zê* only occurs right before *sînay* twice in the Old Testament: Ps 68:8 and Judg 5:5.[20] This phrase becomes a crucial piece of evidence in arguing that Psalm 68 alludes to Judges 5.[21]

First Kings 12:28 presents another example. Jeroboam I wants to avoid people from his newly minted northern kingdom traveling to the rival southern kingdom's Jerusalem Temple, so he makes "two golden

---

that contain the words together. While it remains possible that the words occur in the same passage but not in the same verse, this search function is a great place to start in locating phrases and closely clustered terms.

[17] *The Godfather Part II*, directed by Francis Ford Coppola (Paramount Pictures, 1974).

[18] *Jerry Maguire*, directed by Cameron Crowe (TriStar Pictures, 1996).

[19] Leonard writes, "Shared phrases suggest a stronger connection than do individual shared terms." Leonard, "Identifying Inner-Biblical Allusions," 252.

[20] The phrase is translated broadly, either as a reference to the Lord (i.e., "the One of Sinai" ESV; see CSB also) or in reference to Sinai (i.e., "Sinai itself" NASB; see RSV also).

[21] Psalm 68 alludes to Judges 5 so extensively that Michael Shepherd writes, "It is likely then that Psalm 68 is a reading of Judges 5. . . . From beginning to end Psalm 68 never quite departs from the very specific and unique wording of the text of Judges 5." Michael Shepherd, *The Text in the Middle*, StBibLit 162 (Peter Lang, 2014), 110, 113. For an extended discussion of the many allusions to Judges 5 in Psalm 68, see chapter 2 in my book *From Recollection to Recommitment*, BBR Dissertation Series 1 (Gorgias, 2024).

calves" (v. 28). They are even conveniently located (v. 29), because idolatry is always more convenient than biblical worship. The words "calves" (Hebrew, *ʿēḡel*) and "gold" (Hebrew, *zāhāḇ*) are not determinative on their own. The word *ʿēḡel* occurs 35 times in the Old Testament, and *zāhāḇ* occurs 389 times. As a phrase, though, they appear together only in Exod 32:24; 1 Kgs 12:28; 2 Kgs 10:29; and 2 Chron 13:8. Because 2 Kgs 10:29 and 2 Chron 13:8 both look back to what Jeroboam I did in 1 Kgs 12:28,[22] the source text for 1 Kgs 12:28 is almost certainly Exod 32:24. Exodus 32:24 presents Aaron's attempt to explain how his babysitting of Israel devolved into idolatry. The writer of 1–2 Kings wants readers to know that Jeroboam I's sin recapitulates the nation's original sin, and he signals this by using a unique phrase.

3) Yes, in Unique Clusters of Terms

So far, it might sound like Old Testament writers were consulting a list of Hebrew words or phrases to make sure they only used uncommon ones when referring to another text.[23] Old Testament writers did not know what words or phrases would be rare once the Old Testament canon was complete. They simply made sure to use enough words to nudge an educated reader to the intended source text. So, common terms can help identify an allusion but usually only when clustered together into combinations that were unique to the source text.[24] The technical term for clusters of words is **collocation** (think, co-location, or being located together).

---

[22] Daniel Allen Hutchison, "Exodus in 2 Chronicles 10–36: An Exegetical Study on Inner-Biblical Allusion," (PhD diss., Stellenbosch University, 2021), 60.

[23] James Nogalski argues that "one cannot simply assume that an author could not allude to another text(s) using only uncommon words." Nogalski, "Intertextuality," 109–10.

[24] See Derek D. Bass, "Hosea's Use of Scripture: An Analysis of His Hermeneutics," (PhD diss., Southern Baptist Theological Seminary, 2008), 101; Leonard, "Identifying Inner-Biblical Allusions," 246.

Clusters are different from phrases because the terms occur in the same context but not right next to one another. For example, Ps 106:34–46 narrates the tumultuous era of the judges. Sprinkled through the narration are four fairly common words: *prostitute* as a verbal metaphor for idolatry (v. 39; Hebrew, *zānâ*; 93x in the OT), *enemy* (v. 42; Hebrew, *ʾōyēḇ*; 282x in the OT), *rescue* (v. 43; Hebrew, *nāṣal*; 213x in the OT), and *remember* (v. 45; Hebrew, *zāḵar*; 233x in the OT). None of these are rare words. The only other passage, however, that uses these four words together occurs at the end of Gideon's life: "When Gideon died, the Israelites turned and prostituted [*zānâ*] themselves by worshiping the Baals and made Baal-berith their god. The Israelites did not remember [*zāḵar*] the LORD their God who had rescued [*nāṣal*] them from the hand of the enemies [*ʾōyēḇ*] around them" (Judg 8:33–34). These otherwise common words join forces to allow the psalmist to allude to a specific narrative in Judges.

One more example demonstrates the use of clusters. In Mal 1:6–2:9, the prophet's disputation exposes Judah's priests for allowing disrespectful sacrifices in the temple. Malachi says, "Bring it to your governor! Would he be pleased with you or show you favor?" (Mal 1:8b). They were "profaning" the Lord's name by approaching him in ways they would not approach a human authority (v. 12). So, in Mal 1:8a, Malachi asks, "When you present a blind [*ʿiûēr*] animal for sacrifice, is it not wrong? And when you present a lame [*pissēaḥ*] or sick animal, is it not wrong?" The two-word cluster, "blind" (*ʿiûēr*) and "lame" (*pissēaḥ*), only occurs together in the same verse six times in the Old Testament other than Mal 1:8. The other texts are Lev 21:18; Deut 15:21; 2 Sam 5:6, 8; Job 29:15; and Jer 31:8. There are two ways to narrow down the list. One is to see which text has the most themes in common with Mal 1:8—an approach we will discuss in the next chapter.[25] The other way to narrow down

[25] Following that strategy narrows the potential source text list to Deut 15:21 because, as Jonathan Gibson notes, most of those texts are talking about blind and disabled people rather than animals. Jonathan Gibson, *Covenant Continuity*

the list, in this case, is to widen the cluster of words. Malachi 1:8 and Deut 15:21 both use the relatively common Old Testament verb "sacrifice" (*zāḇaḥ*). Searching all three terms—"blind" (*ʿiûēr*), "lame" (*pisséaḥ*), and "sacrifice" (*zāḇaḥ*)—reveals that this cluster occurs only in two Old Testament texts: Mal 1:8 and Deut 15:21. The Levites under Malachi's microscope were not being vaguely disrespectful. They were committing specific covenant infractions against texts like Deut 15:21: "But if there is a defect in the animal, if it is lame or blind or has any serious defect, you may not sacrifice it to the Lord your God." Malachi uses this allusion to prove that the Levites were not merely breaking decorum, they were breaking Deuteronomic law.

Begin Building the Case with Terms

To summarize, identifying Old Testament allusions begins with terms. English terms, common terms, or stock phrases do not make strong anchors. Rare Hebrew terms, uncommon Hebrew phrases, and clustered Hebrew terms do make strong anchors. Before turning to examples, a note about the way Hebrew terms behave is needed. English words have root words. *Governor* and *government* share the root word, *govern*. Hebrew words also have root words, but the unique element is that root words are usually composed of three consonants (known as **triconsonantal** roots).[26] Nouns, verbs, and adjectives can all flow from the same three-consonant root. "For an example," writes G. Douglas Young,

> the consonants *m-l-k* carry the idea of ruling or reigning. With changes of vowels between the consonants, with the addition

---

and Fidelity: A Study of Inner-Biblical Allusion and Exegesis in Malachi, LHBOTS 625 (Bloomsbury, 2016), 88.

[26] G. Douglas Young explains that "one of the basic structural features" of Hebrew is that "a given concept is carried by three consonants." G. Douglas Young, "The Language of the Old Testament," *EBC* 1 (Zondervan, 1979), 198.

> of prefixes and suffixes, or with both, various related ideas are expressed. In Hebrew, *meleḵ* is "a king"; *melāḵîm*, "kings"; *malḵêhem*, "their kings"; *yimlōḵ*, "he will rule"; *māleḵāh*, "she ruled"; *himlîḵ*, "he caused to reign"; *mamlāḵāh*, "kingdom"; *malḵût*, "royalty"; etc.[27]

All of the terms Young lists have three letters in common (*m-l-k*), pointing to their common root. Why does this matter for Old Testament allusions? Sometimes a text alludes to a source text using not the same term as it appears in a concordance, dictionary, or lexicon, but with the same root that would constitute a different dictionary entry. You may need to recognize that three-consonant root the alluding text borrowed from the source text and tailored grammatically to its purposes.[28]

Micah 7:18–19 does this while alluding to Exod 34:6–7. A student of mine was studying this allusion for an assignment and saw that Mic 7:19's phrase "have compassion" (*rāḥam*) does not occur in Exod 34:6–7. Instead, he noticed that Exod 34:6 uses the adjective "compassionate" (*raḥûm*). This is a separate word in the search tool he was using (Blue Letter Bible), so he did not think it constituted one of the terms Micah 7 uses from Exodus 34. But what consonants do *rāḥam* and *raḥûm* have in common? They share the root *r-ḥ-m*. So, this shared root counts as evidence that Mic 7:18–19 alludes to Exod 34:6–7, but the student needed to know what to look for to recognize the evidence.

An Example of Terms Forming a Weak Anchor

Sometimes I really want a proposed allusion to work, and the following example is one of those. Some time ago, Ulrike Bail proposed that Psalm 55 be read as the prayer of Tamar after the unspeakable crimes of her brother

---

[27] Young, "Language of the Old Testament," 198.

[28] The lexicons available through resources such as Logos, the Blue Letter Bible, or the STEP Bible will allow you to determine whether or not the words you are comparing share a Hebrew root.

in 2 Samuel 13.[29] As a part of that larger argument, Bail proposes an allusion to Judges 19. She asserts that a cluster of three Hebrew words function as a "marker" pointing to the story of horrendous violence in Judges 19 (see chapter 1).[30] The terms in her proposed allusion are underlined here:

Psalm 55:9–11 ALLUDING TEXT (?)	Judges 19:20–22 SOURCE TEXT
Lord, confuse and confound their speech, for I see violence and strife in the city [*ʿîr*]; day and night they make the rounds [*sāḇaḇ*] on its walls. Crime and trouble are within it; destruction is inside it; oppression and deceit never leave its marketplace [*rᵊḥōḇ*].	"Welcome!" said the old man. "I'll take care of everything you need. Only don't spend the night in the square [*rᵊḥōḇ*]."[31] So he brought him to his house and fed the donkeys. Then they washed their feet and ate and drank. While they were enjoying themselves, all of a sudden, wicked men of the city [*ʿîr*] surrounded [*sāḇaḇ*] the house and beat on the door.[32] They said to the old man who was the owner of the house, "Bring out the man who came to your house so we can have sex with him!"

The word *ʿîr* ("city") occurs in the Old Testament 1,092 times. The word *sāḇaḇ* ("move around" or "surround") occurs in the Old Testament 161 times. These are common terms, but *rᵊḥōḇ* ("marketplace" or "public square") is less so at 43 occurrences in the Old Testament. These terms do

---

[29] Ulrike Bail, "The Breath After the Comma, Psalm 55 and Violence Against Women," *Journal of Religion & Abuse* 1, no. 3 (1999): 5–18. On the applicational benefit of Bail's argument, see John Goldingay, *Psalms*, BCOTWP 2 (Baker Academic, 2007), 179.

[30] Bail, "Breath After the Comma," 12.

[31] The passage also uses *rᵊḥōḇ* in verses 15 and 17.

[32] The passage also uses *ʿîr* in verses 11, 12, 15, and 17.

not occur in a phrase together, so the next place to look would be the passages where all three of these words occur together (their cluster or collocation in other Old Testament passages). In addition to Psalm 55 and Judges 19, there are three other passages that contain all three words (for five passages total). The first is Genesis 19 (Sodom and Gomorrah). The presence of these three words in Genesis 19 should not surprise readers of this book, because chapter 1 briefly discussed Judges 19's use of Genesis 19.[33]

The second text is 2 Chronicles 29. There, King Hezekiah gathers spiritual leaders in the "public square," or *rᵊḥōḇ* (v. 4) to get the temple back on track. He explains the need to address temple disrepair and misuse by confessing that their forefathers had "turned . . . away [*sāḇaḇ*] from the Lord (v. 6). This is a different connotation for *sāḇaḇ* than the one in Psalm 55, because the word can connote a variety of literal or figurative movements.[34] The priests and Levites agree and get the temple back in working order (2 Chron 29:12–19). Hezekiah then gathers "city [*'îr*] officials" to make sacrifices at the newly repaired temple (v. 20). Second Chronicles 29 demonstrates my main concern with anchoring an allusion to the cluster of these three terms: most cities (*'îr*) in the ancient world had a public square (*rᵊḥōḇ*). Pairing these words together is as unremarkable as pairing "suburb" and "Target" in twenty-first-century America. The pairing of "city" and "public square," then, appears to be an example of *stock language*.[35]

---

[33] Although what I say later on will make this less likely, it would make more sense for the psalmist to have alluded to Genesis 19 than Judges 19 because of the same shared terms and the theme of confusing the assailants in Ps 55:9 and Gen 19:11. Bail seemingly opts for Judges 19 instead of Genesis 19 because of her wider argument about violence against women that occurs in the former but is only threatened in the latter (Gen 19:8).

[34] The main three connotations are turning around, moving around, or surrounding. Francis Brown, Samuel Rolles Driver, and Charles Augustus Briggs, *Enhanced Brown-Driver-Briggs Hebrew and English Lexicon* (Clarendon, 1977), 685.

[35] There are ten passages in addition to Psalm 55 and Judges 19 that pair these words together: 2 Sam 21:12; 2 Chr 32:6; Esth 4:6; 6:9, 11; Job 29:7; Song 3:2; Jer 5:1; Lam 2:11, 12; and Zech 8:4, 5 (2x).

The third text is Song 3:1–3. The smitten woman says,

> In my bed at night I sought the one I love; I sought him, but did not find him. I will arise now and go about [*sāḇaḇ*] the city [*ʿîr*], through the streets and the plazas [*rᵊḥōḇ*]. I will seek the one I love. I sought him, but did not find him. The guards who go about [*sāḇaḇ*] the city [*ʿîr*] found me. I asked them, "Have you seen the one I love?"

The takeaway from 2 Chronicles is present here too: cities (*ʿîr*) and public squares (*rᵊḥōḇ*) are terms one would expect to find together because the former contained the latter. But Song of Songs 3 demonstrates that moving around (*sāḇaḇ*) is something a lot of people do in cities. This seems like a stock collocation as well because *ʿîr* and *sāḇaḇ* occur together in fourteen Old Testament verses.[36]

A good counterargument would be to assert that *sāḇaḇ* in Judges 19 connotes *surrounding* rather than *moving around*. Some English translations portray *sāḇaḇ* in Psalm 55 as "surrounding" (e.g., GNT, WYC), although this is not the dominant way to translate *sāḇaḇ* in Psalm 55 (cf., CSB, ESV, NASB, NET, NIV). But even if "surround" is the connotation in Psalm 55, this is not unique to Judges 19. In Jeremiah 50, the prophet writes, "Summon the archers to Babylon, all who string the bow; camp all around [*sāḇîḇ*] her; let none escape. . . . Therefore, her young men will fall in her public squares [*rᵊḥōḇ*]; all the warriors will perish in that day. . . . I will set fire to his cities [*ʿîr*], and it will consume everything around [*sāḇîḇ*] him" (vv. 29a, 30a, 32b). The word *sāḇîḇ* in Jeremiah 50 comes from the same Hebrew root as *sāḇaḇ* in Psalm 55. Jeremiah 50:29–32 demonstrates the stock nature of the terms Bail says are markers pointing to Judges 19. Cities have squares, and cities were often surrounded. That's

[36] These passages do not include Psalm 55 and Judges 19 and are Josh 6:3, 4, 7, 14, 15 (2x), 16; Judg 16:2; 2 Kgs 6:15; 2 Chr 14:7; 17:9; Pss 48:12; 59:6, 14; and Song 3:2.

how cities were defeated. If indeed the shared terms between Psalm 55 and Judges 19 are a stock cluster, then the anchor for this proposed allusion does not hold.[37]

An Example of Terms Forming a Strong Anchor

This example showcases terms and phrases. Look at this side-by-side comparison:

Psalm 113:7–9 ALLUDING TEXT	1 Samuel 2:5, 8 SOURCE TEXT
He raises [*qûm*] the poor (*dal*) from the dust (*ʿāp̄ār*) and lifts (*rûm*) the needy (*eḇyôn*) from the trash [*ašpōṯ*] heap [*ʿāp̄ār*] in order to seat [*yāšaḇ*] them with nobles [*nāḏîḇ*]—with the nobles of his people. He gives the childless woman [*ʿāqār*] a household, making her the joyful mother of children. Hallelujah!	Those who are full hire themselves out for food, but those who are starving hunger no more. The woman who is childless [*ʿāqār*] gives birth to seven, but the woman with many sons pines away. . . . He raises [*qûm*] the poor [*dal*] from the dust [*ʿāp̄ār*] and lifts [*rûm*] the needy [*eḇyôn*] from the trash [*ašpōṯ*] heap [*ʿāp̄ār*]. He seats [*yāšaḇ*] them with noblemen [*nāḏîḇ*] and gives them a throne of honor. For the foundations of the earth are the Lord's; he has set the world on them.

[37] John Kselman and Michael Barré assess Bail's overall argument, and I think it applies to her subpoint about Psalm 55 and Judges 19, by saying, "While this reading is not impossible, neither is it compelling, given the absence of explicit evidence in Psalm 55 supporting the claim." John S. Kselman and Michael L. Barré, "Psalm 55: Problems and Proposals," *CBQ* 60, no. 3 (1998), 440n1.

What makes this a strong anchor? First, both texts share a rare word. The term for a woman unable to have children (*ʿāqār*) only occurs twelve times in the Old Testament. Second, the texts both contain nine Hebrew words in the same order—an extended version of the phrase criteria explained in this chapter. The source text occurs in Hannah's Song (1 Sam 2:1–10). In this allusion, the psalmist shows that it is one thing to say God exalts the lowly, but it is another thing to cite a specific instance when it occurs. Alluding to Hannah's Song adds concreteness to the reasons for praise in Psalm 113. This allusion also offers readers solidarity with previous generations of God's people.[38]

Conclusion

Renee Ballard, Michael Connelly's fictional cold case detective, discussed evidence in a case and complained that "these [other kinds of evidence] don't get priority like DNA from crime scenes."[39] Terms function this way in Scripture's use of Scripture. They are the first and foundational connection when the source text and alluding text share uncommon Hebrew words, uncommon Hebrew phrases, and uncommon clusters of Hebrew words. More evidence will be needed, but it all starts with terms.

---

[38] Daniel J. Estes, *Psalms 73–150*, NAC 13 (B&H, 2019), 361.

[39] Michael Connelly, *The Waiting* (Little, Brown, 2024), 18.

4

Instinct 2: Themes—Confirm the Allusion

Introduction

It was the golden age of Adam Sandler. As middle schoolers at a Christian school, though, our parents did not all view it as a cinematic golden age. My two friends and I represented the spectrum of late-'90s Christian media consumption. One friend, let's call him Drew, could watch nearly everything (and his parents had the coveted satellite dish). The other, let's call him Jeremy, could watch almost nothing. I occupied the middle—allowed to watch more than Jeremy but not *Braveheart* like Drew. I think Jeremy and I both envied Drew's freedom, and Jeremy was slightly sheepish about his parents' strictness. While analyzing the latest Adam Sandler movie, Jeremy would discuss the movie and even quote it without letting on that he had not seen the film. After a while, we noticed that all his quotes had one thing in common: they were in the movie commercials (Gen Z, this was like a YouTube movie trailer that aired on TV). When asked, he would admit, "No, I haven't seen it, but I did see the commercial." He was able to reference the film if the quotes or scenes were portrayed in the preview but fell silent when references ventured to the rest of the film. After a while, Drew and I became rather adept at determining if Jeremy was quoting the film or quoting an advertisement.[1]

Jeremy lacked what Richard Schultz calls "**contextual awareness**," or elements that the alluding and source texts share beyond the wording of the allusion or quotation.[2] When Drew referred to a line from *Happy Gilmore*, he assumed the listener knew the preceding and following scenes well enough to grasp the significance of the movie line. Likewise, in Scripture, "a knowledge of the quoted text . . . is assumed by the speaker or author."[3] Biblical authors not only assumed that an ideal reader knew something about the context being alluded to but also probably had the source text in mind for longer than it took to pen the exact words in the allusion. Unlike college freshmen who Google-hunt a quote and then do not think about it again, biblical authors selected source texts for their quotations and allusions based on deep meditation superintended by the Holy Spirit. Just as broader scenes or themes from a film showed whether Jeremy was alluding to the film or preview, so broader themes or elements shared by an alluding and source text substantiate *if* and *how* the alluding text employs the source text. The most relevant evidence of contextual awareness is, as the name of this chapter suggests, *themes*. Confirmation and appreciation of allusions comes when a potential alluding text shares themes with a potential source text.[4]

---

[1] For what it's worth, my kids' media consumption is a lot more like Jeremy's than mine or Drew's.

[2] Richard L. Schultz, *The Search for Quotation: Verbal Parallels in the Prophets*, JSOTSS 180 (Sheffield Academic, 1999), 224.

[3] Schultz, 224.

[4] Derek Bass boils contextual awareness down to two elements: "thematic or structural links." Derek D. Bass, "The Use of the Old Testament in the Old Testament: Reassessing Hosea 6:7 in Light of Hosea's Pervasive Use of Genesis," in *The Law, the Prophets, and the Writings: Studies in Evangelical Old Testament Hermeneutics in Honor of Duane A. Garrett* (B&H Academic, 2021), 204. We

How to Determine Shared Themes and Why They Matter for Allusion Identification

Before explaining the two main reasons for the *themes* instinct, I want to explain how to detect shared themes in two biblical texts. I confessed in chapter 2 my love for the fiction writer Michael Connelly. His flagship protagonist—whom I followed long before he became a hit Amazon Original series staple—is veteran LAPD detective Harry Bosch. Harry Bosch is an amalgam of the investigators Michael Connelly encountered when he was a journalist covering crime in Florida and Los Angeles. One real-life investigator, George Hurt, displayed a sign in the detective squad room, and Connelly wrote that sign into the minimal decor on Bosch's fictional desk. The sign contains a mantra that epitomizes painstaking investigative work: "Get off your [posterior] and knock on doors."[5] Staring only at crime scenes may not solve cases (though perhaps it does sometimes). The *context* of the crime needs to be scoured for the insight, leads, and tidbits that might lead detectives to solve a crime. Likewise, whereas instinct one (terms) deals with the narrow components of an allusion, instinct two (themes) gets out into the wider neighborhood of the two texts involved and knocks on doors. The wider neighborhood of the alluding and source texts are what G. K. Beale calls their "immediate" and "broad" contexts.[6] The **immediate context** refers to each text's paragraph or poetic stanza, and the **broad context** refers

deal in this chapter with the first, but the second refers to instances where the alluding text has a grammatical or even a wider structuring feature in common with the source text.

[5] Michael Connelly, *Crime Beat: A Decade of Covering Cops and Killers* (Little, Brown, 2006), 29.

[6] Here I draw on the wording of steps 2–3 in G. K. Beale's nine steps for analyzing the NT use of the OT: "Analyze the broad NT context where the OT reference occurs" (in our case, that would be the context of the alluding OT passage) and "Analyze the OT context both broadly and immediately, especially thoroughly interpreting the paragraph in which the quotation or allusion

at least to the chapter(s) containing the allusion.[7] Comb through the contexts of the alluding and source texts and then note the overlapping themes. Some themes are virtually everywhere in the Old Testament, like God and sin. Some themes are less common and can help confirm an allusion.[8] Common or not, the wider the net the better.[9] With that, here are two primary outcomes for this second instinct and examples of their usefulness.

---

occurs." G. K. Beale, *Handbook on the New Testament Use of the Old Testament: Exegesis and Interpretation* (Baker Academic, 2012), 43–44.

[7] Looking beyond the chapter divisions themselves to the section of the book that contains the alluding and source texts is always fruitful.

[8] Dane Ortlund provides one of the best examples I have seen of this kind of confirmatory work. He argues that in Luke 24:31, when the two disciples on the road to Emmaus ate with Jesus and had their eyes opened, Luke alludes to Adam and Eve eating and having their eyes opened in Gen 3:7. After Ortlund makes the case on the level of terms, he turns to what he calls "narratival" evidence, or elements shared by each narrative. They are worth listing here to demonstrate the type of thinking required in this chapter: (1) a pair of humans (Gen 3:6; Luke 24:13); (2) food offered to the pair (Gen 3:1–5; Luke 24:30); (3) a supernatural being offering the food (Gen 3:1–5; Luke 24:52); (4) the unexpected nature of the offer of food (i.e., the intruder or guest offering the food) (Gen 3:1; Luke 24:29–30); (5) acceptance of the food (Gen 3:6; Luke 24:30–31); (6) the humans do not recognize the offeror's identity (Gen 3:1–7; Luke 24:16); (7) new perception after eating (Gen 3:7–10; Luke 24:32); (8) same phrase describes the new perception, (i.e., the wording of the allusion) (Gen 3:7; Luke 24:31); (9) previous divine revelation is newly grasped (Gen 3:7; Luke 24:32); (10) spatial separation from God after eating (Gen 3:8; Luke 24:31); (11) God comes to the people, initially resulting in fear (Gen 3:9–12; Luke 24:36–41); (12) the human pair travels (Gen 3:23; Luke 24:33). Dane C. Ortlund, "'And Their Eyes Were Opened, and They Knew': An Inter-Canonical Note on Luke 24:31," *JETS* 53, no. 4 (2010): 725.

[9] Ziva Ben-Porat says, "Regardless of the varying importance" of the connections, they assist in identifying the maximum comprehensive relationship between the alluding and source texts. Ziva Ben-Porat, "The Poetics of Literary Allusion," *PTL: A Journal for Descriptive Poetics and Theory of Literature* 1 (1976): 111.

1) Confirm the Allusion

The first outcome is to confirm what the first instinct—terms—unearthed, or to confirm the allusion. For example, Ps 68:12 uses the phrase "divides the spoil." "Divide" (Hebrew, *ḥālaq*) occurs fifty-five times in the Old Testament, and "spoil" (Hebrew, *šālāl*) occurs seventy-five times. That is not a rare phrase, but neither term effectively narrows down a potential source text. Recall from chapter 3 that the uniqueness of a phrase or word cluster is the next place to look. Paired together as a subject and verb, however, the words *ḥālaq* and *šālāl* only occur ten times in the Old Testament. Among the ten is Judg 5:30. This is probably the source text because of the number of themes the contexts share. Beginning with the immediate contexts, the poetic stanzas in Ps 68:11–14 and Judg 5:28–30:

1. Both involve women: female messengers in Ps 68:11 and both Sisera's mother and her attendants in Judg 5:28–29.
2. Both involve news from the battlefield: from the women heralds in Ps 68:11 and Sisera's mother wondering why the report has not yet arrived in Judg 5:28.
3. Both involve kings at war: generic enemies of Israel in Ps 68:12, 14 and Sisera the enemy of Deborah and Barak in Judg 5:28.
4. Both, as the terms of the allusion suggest, involve plunder: general plunder in Ps 68:11–13 and the dehumanizing, gaudy plunder Sisera's mother expected in Judg 5:30.

The broad contexts of each passage, in this case their single poetic chapters, include the following themes in common:

1. Both contexts engage in praise through song (Ps 68:4, 19, 26, 32, 35; Judg 5:1–3, 9).
2. Both contexts contain water imagery (Ps 68:8–9; Judg 5:4–5, 21).
3. Both contexts involve the shaming of evil kings (Ps 68:12, 29; Judg 5:3, 19).
4. Both contexts contain mountain imagery (Ps 68:15–16; Judg 5:5).

5. Both contexts present the Lord as a warrior (Ps 68:7–8; Judg 5:4–5).
6. Both contexts show God's grace to humble or weak people (Ps 68:4–5; Judg 5:6–7).
7. Both contexts rebuke those who do not participate in the Lord's battles (Ps 68:13; Judg 5:16).[10]

None of these themes is exclusive to Psalm 68 and Judges 5, but together they build a cumulative case that supports what the shared phrase already suggested.

2) Look for Additional, Clarifying Connections

The second outcome from the *themes* instinct is more interpretive than the first outcome and asks, Could there be additional connections between the alluding and source texts that clarify the relationship between the two texts?[11] If indeed God wanted one biblical text to refer to another biblical text, this step opens up the interpreter to the full range of conversation between the two texts. Sometimes, as in the Psalm 68 and Judges 5 example, the result is finding additional allusions to the source text. By my count, Psalm 68 alludes to Judges 5 eight times (including the example on page 63).[12] Many of the allusions may not have been noticed by interpreters if the most famous of the allusions—more of a quotation because of its length (Ps 68:7–8//Judg 5:4–5)—had not prompted scholars to cast a wider net into additional connections between the texts.

---

[10] Matthew E. Swale, *From Recollection to Recommitment: The Rhetorical Function of Allusions to Judges in Psalms 68, 83, and 106*, BBR Dissertation Series 1 (Gorgias, 2024), 55–57.

[11] Ben-Porat describes this as the "[a]ctivation of the evoked text (RT) as a whole, in an attempt to form maximum intertextual patterns." Ben-Porat, "The Poetics of Literary Allusion," 111.

[12] Swale, *From Recollection to Recommitment*, 50.

Even if there are not additional allusions, combing for shared themes provides clues to the biblical author's purpose for the allusion. Robert Chisholm provides a meaningful example in Hab 1:8. Habakkuk masterfully weaves prior biblical texts into his book, so one's allusion antennae should be on high alert when reading him. Describing the (shocking) plan of God to use the Babylonians, the Lord tells Habakkuk, "Their horses are swifter than leopards / and more fierce than wolves of the night. / Their horsemen charge ahead; / their horsemen come from distant lands. / They fly like eagles, swooping to devour" (Hab 1:8). The English phrase "from distant lands" is a compound word in Hebrew, *merāḥôq*, comprised of a prefix that means "from" (*me-*) and a noun (*rāḥôq*) that is often translated as "afar" in this verse (e.g., RSV, NIV, NASB, ESV). Chisholm argues that Habakkuk alludes to Deut 28:49: "The Lord will bring a nation from far away [*merāḥôq*], from the ends of the earth, to swoop down on you like an eagle, a nation whose language you won't understand."[13]

What else do Hab 1:8 and Deut 28:49 have in common? We begin with the immediate contexts, Hab 1:5–11 and Deut 28:45–51:

1. Both texts compare enemies to eagles (Hab 1:8; Deut 28:49).[14]
2. Both texts pertain to enemy nations (Hab 1:5–6; Deut 28:48).
3. Both texts mention the violence of the enemy nations (Hab 1:7; Deut 28:50).
4. Both texts contain extensive animal references and imagery (Hab 1:8; Deut 28:49, 51).
5. Both texts reveal a shocking act of God against his people (Hab 1:5–6; Deut 28:46).

[13] Robert B. Chisholm Jr., "Book of Habakkuk," *Dictionary of the New Testament Use of the Old Testament* (Baker Academic, 2023), 284–85.

[14] This is technically another term (Instinct 1), rather than a theme alone (Instinct 2), because both texts use the Hebrew word *nešer*.

Then the broader contexts, Habakkuk 1–3 and Deuteronomy 28,[15] share the themes in the next list. It is worth noting that Deuteronomy 28 is one of the most important passages in the Mosaic covenant due to its description of the blessings Israel will receive for covenant faithfulness and the curses Israel will receive for covenant unfaithfulness:

1. Both contexts concern God's law (Hab 1:4; Deut 28:1, 15).
2. Both contexts highlight faith or faithfulness (Hab 2:4; Deut 28:1, 15).
3. Both contexts highlight covenant unfaithfulness (Hab 1:2–3; Deut 28:15, 45).
4. Both contexts describe agricultural failure (Hab 3:17; Deut 28:17, 39–40).

These wider connections allow readers to see why Hab 1:8 brings Deuteronomy 28 into the conversation: "The Babylonian invasion implements the threatened judgments (i.e., 'curses') against those who have broken their covenant with the Lord (cf. Hab. 1:4)."[16] Without knowledge of, or investigation of, the contexts of Habakkuk and Deuteronomy 28, the reader risks missing the broader overlap Habakkuk wants readers to see with the source text.

When Themes Make a Difference

Three scenarios receive significant help from *themes*. The first scenario is when the *terms* are unimpressive or inconclusive. For example, Barry Webb is convinced that when Samson eats honey from a lion's carcass in Judges 14—probably a forbidden touch for someone under a Nazirite

---

[15] The reason for the wider net here is that the whole book of Habakkuk contains a few hundred words less than Deuteronomy 28.

[16] Chisholm, "Book of Habakkuk," 285.

vow (Num 6:6; Judg 13:5)—the narrator wants readers to know that this was not the "purely innocent act" it appears to be on the surface.[17] The description of Samson seeing, taking, eating (a forbidden spread), and giving some to his parents (Judg 14:8–9) possesses intentional "resonance" with Eve's actions in Genesis 3.[18] Here are the texts side by side:[19]

Judges 14:7–9 ALLUDING TEXT	Genesis 3:6 SOURCE TEXT
Then he went and spoke to the woman, because she seemed right to Samson [literally, she was right in the eyes (*ʿayin*) of Samson]. After some time, when he returned to marry her, he left the road to see [*rāʾâ*] the lion's carcass, and there was a swarm of bees with honey in the carcass. He scooped some honey into his hands and ate [*ʾāḵal*] it as he went along. When he came to his father and mother, he gave [*nāṯan*] some to them and they ate it. But he did not tell them that he had scooped the honey from the lion's carcass.	The woman saw [*rāʾâ*] that the tree was good for food and delightful to look at [*ʿayin*], and that it was desirable for obtaining wisdom. So she took some of its fruit and ate [*ʾāḵal*] it; she also gave [*nāṯan*] some to her husband, who was with her, and he ate [*ʾāḵal*] it.

Because *ʿayin* (eyes) and *ʾāḵal* (eat) occur over 800 times each and *rāʾâ* (see) and *nāṯan* (give) occur about 1,300 times and 2,000 times respectively, the overlap of terms is either inconclusive or unimpressive. Since

[17] Barry G. Webb, *The Book of Judges*, NICOT (Eerdmans, 2012), 369.

[18] Webb, 369.

[19] Although I have added Judg 14:7 because of the term *eyes*, this side-by-side comparison comes from Jillian L. Ross, "Type-Casting the Samson Family: Genesis Parodies in Judges 13–14," *JETS* 64, no. 2 (2021): 251.

people *see* with their eyes and often *give* people something to eat, these similarities could be considered stock phrases. Jillian Ross concludes that since the "verbal parallels are sparse . . . the relationship between the two texts is largely thematic."[20]

What are the thematic links? We begin with the immediate contexts, Judg 14:5–9 and Gen 3:1–7, sharing these themes:

1. Both texts involve animals (Gen 3:1; Judg 14:5).
2. Both texts involve retrieving food (Gen 3:6; Judg 14:9).[21]
3. Both scenes occur in a cultivated agricultural context (Gen 3:2; Judg 14:5).[22]
4. Both texts follow the same sequence: see, retrieve, eat, and give (Gen 3:6; Judg 14:8–9).[23]

Next, the two broader contexts of each passage (Gen 2:18–3:24 and Judg 13:25–15:6) share these themes:

1. Both contexts involve marriage (Gen 2:24; Judg 14:1–4).
2. Both contexts involve cunning words (Gen 3:1–2; Judg 14:12).
3. Both contexts involve promising starts (Gen 2:18–25; Judg 13:25).

[20] Ross, 251.

[21] *Take* (*lāqaḥ*) in Gen 3:6 and *scoop* (*rāḏâ*) in Judg 14:9.

[22] *Garden* (*gan*) in Genesis 3 and *vineyard* (*kerem*) in Judg 14:5–9.

[23] This fourth similarity is another form of contextual awareness that we are not focusing on in this chapter but one of which it is good to be aware. Sometimes a biblical author alludes to a source text by mirroring its structure or flow. Chapter 1 demonstrated how Judges 19 does this with Genesis 19, for example. Jeffery Leonard calls this "narrative tracking," because one text is "mimicking" the structure of the other. Jeffery M. Leonard, "Identifying Subtle Allusions: The Promise of Narrative Tracking," *Subtle Citation, Allusion, and Translation in the Hebrew Bible* (Equinox, 2017), 97.

4. Both contexts involve transgressing a command that someone in the narrative restates (Gen 3:3; Judg 14:3).[24]
5. Both contexts involve clothing (Gen 3:21; Judg 14:13).
6. Both contexts involve marital blame (Gen 3:12; Judg 14:16, 18b).
7. Both contexts involve fire (Gen 3:24; Judg 14:15; 15:5–6).

The number of themes shared by the immediate and broad contexts of Samson's eating and Eve's eating supports Ross's claim that Samson is not only a "type of Eve" but, given his self-deception compared to Eve's deception by the serpent, Samson "failed to heed Scripture . . . and acted in a manner worse than Scripture's first sinners."[25]

The second scenario helped by *themes* is when more than one potential source text exists. Greater thematic similarity with one of the potential texts narrows down the source text candidates. Earlier in the chapter, the phrase "divides the spoil" in Psalm 68 and Judges 5 led to a list of eleven shared themes between the two texts. I mentioned, however, that there are a total of ten occurrences of the phrase in the Old Testament (including Psalm 68 and Judges 5)—so, why is Judges 5 a more likely source text than the others? One way to address this question is to compare the thematic overlap in a side-by-side chart. The following chart demonstrates how Psalm 68 shares more themes with Judges 5 than with the earliest three texts containing the phrase *divide the spoil* (Gen 49:27; Exod 15:9; Josh 22:8). Begin with the total number of shared themes you detect in the alluding and source texts (e.g., the left column in the sample below), and comb through the other potential source texts to check for these or other shared themes.

---

[24] Samson's parents remind Samson of a covenantal obligation already made prominent in the narration of Judg 3:1–6 and its allusion to Deuteronomy 7.

[25] Ross, "Type-Casting," 252.

Alluding Text	Potential Source Texts			
Psalm 68	Judges 5	Joshua 22	Exodus 15	Genesis 49
Women	X	-	X	-
Battle News	X	-	-	-
Enemy Kings	X	-	X	-
Shame to Kings	X	-	X	-
Plunder	X	X	X	X
Praise	X	X	X	-
Water	X	-	X	X
Mountains	X	-	X	X
Divine Warrior	X	-	X	-
Grace to the Weak	X	-	-	-
Shaming Inactivity	X	-	-	-

Judges 5 comes out on top, even if it does so narrowly compared to Exodus 15. It is possible Judges 5 is influenced by Exodus 15, resulting in the shared themes between Psalm 68 and Exodus 15.[26] The themes missing in Exodus 15 are significant, because there the Lord alone fights

[26] The most noticeable similarity between Judges 5 and Exodus 15 is that they are victory songs paired with a narrative about which they sing praise (Exodus 14–15; Judges 4–5). Robert O'Connell argues extensively that Judges 5 intentionally alludes to Exodus 15 to glorify God as the victor by evoking "the archetypal victory of YHWH over Pharaoh's army." Robert O'Connell, *The Rhetoric of the Book of Judges* (Brill, 1996), 137. Even though calling it an *allusion* is rare, the copious similarities between Judges 5 and Exodus 15 cause scholars to grapple with and variously explain their commonalities (common form, common occasion, etc.). See Alan J. Hauser, "Two Songs of Victory: A Comparison of Exodus 15 and Judges 5," *Directions in Biblical Hebrew Poetry*, JSOTSS 40 (Sheffield Academic, 1987), 265–84.

(Exod 14:14), whereas Judges 5 and Psalm 68 highly encourage human agency in their warfare subject matter.

Because I am convinced David wrote Psalm 68 as the canonical title suggests,[27] the three texts in the chart represent the best rivals to Judges 5 as Psalm 68's source text. Most scholars do not accept Davidic authorship of Psalm 68,[28] however, so it would be wise to use themes to rule out the remaining five texts as the source for Psalm 68 (Prov 16:19; Isa 9:3; 33:23; 53:12; Zech 14:1).

The chart on page 72 demonstrates that, even for those who deny the Davidic authorship of Psalm 68, none of these texts supplant Judges 5 as the most likely source text for Psalm 68.

The third scenario helped by *themes* is when scholars disagree about the presence of an allusion. Sometimes one commentary mentions an allusion in an Old Testament text, and another either does not mention it or outright disagrees. Exploring thematic similarities, or lack thereof, can adjudicate situations like this. Song of Songs presents a fascinating example of this sort of disagreement. Broadly, some theologians argue that the Song does not allude to Scripture at all.[29] By contrast, others contend that

---

[27] For four reasons that David fits the implied speaker in Psalm 68, see Swale, *From Recollection to Recommitment*, 62–64.

[28] A. F. Kirkpatrick's summary of the scholarly situation over a century ago still holds: "Every conceivable occasion and date have been suggested for this Psalm, from the age of Joshua to that of the Maccabees." A. F. Kirkpatrick, *The Book of Psalms* (Cambridge University Press, 1906), 375.

[29] Gary Edward Schnittjer carefully explains that, first, there is no interpretive use of Scripture in the Song; second, there are similarities with other OT texts but most "do not even constitute broad allusion to other Scripture"; third, the most "discussed" similarities with other OT texts are probably better categorized as "cross-references but not interpretive allusions." Gary Edward Schnittjer, *Old Testament Use: A Book-by-Book Guide* (Zondervan, 2021), 591. Miles Van Pelt cites Schnittjer in agreement but only mentions quotations (not allusions): "Song of Songs neither quotes nor is quoted by other Scripture." Miles V. Van Pelt, "Book of Song of Songs," *Dictionary of the New Testament Use of the Old Testament* (Baker Academic, 2023), 799. For a meaningful challenge to the second embedded claim, that the NT does not use the Song, see Christopher W. Mitchell, *The Song of Songs*, Concordia Commentary Series (Concordia, 2003), 29–34.

Alluding Text	Potential Source Texts					
Psalm 68	**Judges 5**	**Proverbs 16:19**	**Isaiah 9**[30]	**Isaiah 33**[31]	**Isaiah 53**[32]	**Zechariah 14**
Women	X	-	-	-	-	-
Battle News	X	-	X	-	-	-
Enemy Kings	X	-	X	-	-	-
Shame to Kings	X	-	X	-	X	-
Plunder	X	X	X	X	X	X
Praise	X	-	X	X	-	X
Water	X	-	X	X	-	X
Mountains	X	-	-	X	-	X
Divine Warrior	X	-	-	-	-	-
Grace to the Weak	X	X	-	X	-	-
Shaming Inactivity	X	-	-	-	-	-

[30] Psalm 68 and Isaiah 9 also share the themes of fatherlessness (Ps 68:5; Isa 9:17) and harvest (Ps 68:9; Isa 9:3).
[31] Psalm 68 and Isaiah 33 also share the theme of God rising (Ps 68:1; Isa 33:10).
[32] The relevant unit spans Isa 52:13–53:12.

the Song cannot be understood without attention for the way its poetry interprets and assumes knowledge of other Scripture through its allusions.[33] These are very different claims.

One of the most convincing potential allusions in the book is in Song 7:10. There the woman says, "I am my love's, and his desire [*tᵊšûqâ*] is for me." The Hebrew word *tᵊšûqâ* only occurs two other times in the Old Testament. The first is in God's disciplinary actions on Adam, Eve, and the serpent. He says to Eve, "Your desire [*tᵊšûqâ*] will be for your husband, yet he will rule over you" (Gen 3:16b). The second is when God warns Cain, "If you do what is right, won't you be accepted? But if you do not do what is right, sin is crouching at the door. Its desire [*tᵊšûqâ*] is for you, but you must rule over it" (4:7). In entertaining the possibility of an allusion, we begin on decent footing with *terms* because *tᵊšûqâ* is a rare Hebrew word in the Old Testament. *Themes*, as we have noted, can help narrow down the potential source texts because Song 7:10 has something in common with Gen 3:16 that it does not have in common with Gen 4:7: marriage. But even here, scholars are divided. Duane Garrett says, "There is little reason to think that [the links] are deliberate allusions to Genesis" and the shared term is of "dubious value."[34] Ellen Davis thinks the shared term is "crucial for understanding

---

[33] James Hamilton writes, "We should read the Song as summarizing and interpreting the big story of the Bible, contributing to it, depicting it in verse." James M. Hamilton Jr., *Song of Songs: A Biblical-Theological, Allegorical, Christological Interpretation* (Christian Focus, 2015), 18. Hamilton seems to be referring to the phenomenon of inner-biblical interpretation or inner-biblical exegesis, a subset of inner-biblical allusion that alludes in order to freshly interpret other biblical texts. Similarly, Ellen Davis argues that the Song is always "assuming that our imaginations have already had some 'training' in biblical tradition" through its use of that tradition. Ellen F. Davis, *Proverbs, Ecclesiastes, and the Song of Songs*, Westminster Bible Companion Series (WJK, 2000), 238.

[34] Duane Garrett and Paul R. House, *Song of Songs and Lamentations*, WBC 23B (Zondervan, 2004), 98–99.

the present passage and the meaning of the Song altogether."[35] Once again, very different claims.

Perhaps *themes* can serve as referee. Starting with the immediate contexts, what themes do Song 7:10–13 and Gen 3:14–19 have in common? At least these:

1. Both texts concern the relationship between a husband and a wife (Song 7:10; Gen 3:12, 17).
2. Both texts share the theme of sexual intercourse or its procreative results (Song 7:12b; Gen 3:16a).
3. Both texts share references to a field (*śāḏê*) (Song 7:11; Gen 3:18).
4. Both texts refer to agricultural harvest (Song 7:12; Gen 3:17–19).

What about the wider contexts of each text (Song 6:4–8:4; Genesis 1–3)? They share these eight themes:

1. Both contexts contain fruit or fruit imagery (Song 7:12; Gen 3:2)
2. Both contexts are set in a garden (*gan*), literally or figuratively (8x in the Song; 13x in Genesis 2–3).[36]
3. Both contexts contain water or water imagery (Gen 2:10–14; Song 7:4).
4. Both contexts contain trees or tree imagery (Gen 2:16–17; Song 6:11; 7:7).
5. Both contexts contain regal imagery (Gen 1:28; Song 7:5).
6. Both contexts contain kinship language (Gen 2:23–25; Song 8:1).[37]

---

[35] Davis, *Proverbs*, 294.

[36] This moves outside of Song 6:4–8:4, but the book setting is relevant to broad context also (especially in shorter compositions like Song of Songs). The word *garden* (*gan*) occurs 42x in the OT, and the two highest frequency books are Genesis (14x) and Song of Songs (8x).

[37] Ken Mathews explains that "bone" and "flesh" in Gen 2:23 occurs later in the OT to refer to kinship and that the marriage of Adam and Eve is described as a "new kinship" in Gen 2:24. Kenneth A. Mathews, *Genesis 1–11:26–50:26*, NAC 1B (B&H, 1996), 223.

7. Both contexts portray nakedness positively, which is a rare thing for Scripture to do (Gen 2:25; Song 7:7–8).[38]
8. Both contexts contain sanctuary imagery suggesting canonical relationships with the tabernacle and temple.[39]

Apprehending themes involves instinct, not scientific method. These twelve themes, however, seem to suggest a relationship between Song 7:10

---

[38] Most other references to nakedness in the Bible either connote shame (Gen 3:7; Rev 3:18), vulnerability (Gen 42:12), destitution (Luke 8:27), or judgment (Nah 3:5). Proverbs 5:19 is a notable exception, which, like the Song, is Solomonic. Paul R. House writes of the lovers in Song of Songs, "Their love recaptures Genesis 2:25 as much as is possible in a sinful world." Paul R. House, *Old Testament Theology* (InterVarsity, 1998), 465.

[39] G. K. Beale suggests eight ways that the later sanctuaries of the OT were cast in Edenic language: (1) God walked about in both (same Hebrew phrase in Gen 3:8; Lev 26:12); (2) the Hebrew words for *serve* and *keep* describe the caretakers of both (Gen 2:15; Num 3:7); (3) the lampstand resembled a tree and was positioned like the tree of life in relation to the holy of holies; (4) extensive wood carvings in the temple (1 Kgs 6:29) resemble the trees of Eden (see Gen 2:9); (5) Eden's position on a mountain (Ezek 28:14) facing east (Gen 3:24) is mirrored in Zion's topography; (6) there were rivers in Eden (Gen 2:10) and in the eschatological temple (Ezek 47:1–12); (7) Eden/temple have three sections in river source/holy of holies, garden/holy place, and outskirts/outer court; (8) Ezek 28:14, 18 describe Eden as a sanctuary. G. K. Beale, "Temple," *Dictionary of the New Testament Use of the Old Testament* (Baker Academic, 2023), 830. Song of Songs contains at least eight images that also exist in Israel's sanctuary settings: (1) the book is associated with the temple-builder King Solomon; (2) "pomegranates" are mentioned 32x in the OT, including 8x in tabernacle décor, 12x in temple décor, and 6x in the Song; (3) "frankincense" is mentioned 21x in the OT, 15x of which are either in sacrificial use, the tabernacle, or the temple, and 3x in the Song; (4) "myrrh" is mentioned 12x in the OT: mostly in the Song (8x) and once in connection with the tabernacle; (5) "palm trees" are mentioned 12x in the OT: 2x in the Song and once in a festal context (Lev 23:40); (6) cedar wood is mentioned 3x in the Song, and 23x in the construction of the temple; (7) Lebanon is mentioned 7x in the Song and 8x in the construction of the temple; (8) lilies are mentioned 15x in the OT: 8x in the Song and 4x in temple décor.

and the Gen 3:16 that is beyond coincidence. But why? Chapter 5 will return to this example to answer that question.

An Example of Themes Ruling Out an Allusion

Back in chapter 2, we considered a brief example of a rare term forming a strong anchor for a proposed allusion. Psalm 29:10 uses the word *flood* (*mabûl*) that only occurs otherwise in the narrative of Noah and the flood (Genesis 6–9). Inspecting the two contexts reveals enough contextual overlap to not challenge the strong case made with the *terms* involved. Sometimes, however, what looks like strong anchor in the *terms* is weakened by a lack of shared *themes*. For example, Jer 10:5 occurs in what scholars call an *anti-idol polemic*, where the prophet roasts the concept of graven images. The prophet says, "Like scarecrows in a cucumber patch, their idols cannot speak" (10:5a). The word translated "scarecrow(s)" comes from a rare Hebrew word (*tōmer*). *Tōmer* also appears in Judg 4:5 where Deborah "would sit under the palm tree [*tōmer*] of Deborah between Ramah and Bethel in the hill country of Ephraim, and the Israelites went up to her to settle disputes." For two texts to possess the only two occurrences of a Hebrew word in the Old Testament would often be strongly indicative of an allusion. But the *themes* reduce the likelihood of an allusion. In Jer 10:5, the *tōmer* is a simile for the laughable inactivity of idols. In Judg 4:5, the *tōmer* is Deborah's literal office space. For this reason, to my knowledge, even the shared rare term does not lead anyone to suggest that Jeremiah is alluding to Judges here. Themes make a difference.

An Example of Themes Substantiating an Allusion

This example serves the point of this chapter well because of the avalanche of themes shared by the two texts. Hava Shalom-Guy offers two pieces of *terms* evidence to argue that the call of Gideon in Judg 6:11–24 alludes to the call of Moses in Exod 3:1–4:17.[40] First, both passages contain the phrase *for* (*kî*) *I am* (*hāyâ*) *with* (*ʿim*) *you* (*-k*) (Exod 3:12; Judg 6:16). Second, both passages contain the word cluster including (1) *see* or *appear* (*rāʾâ*), (2) *angel* (*malʾāḵ*), and (3) *Yahweh* (*Yhwh*) (Exod 3:2; Judg 6:12). On the surface, these may seem like a stock phrase and stock cluster,[41] so the shared themes carry the day. They include:[42]

1. Both texts open with someone doing agricultural work for their father (Judg 6:11) or father-in-law (Exod 3:1).
2. Both texts involve fiery displays of the Lord's power (Exod 3:2; Judg 6:21).
3. Both texts mention Midian (Exod 3:1; Judg 6:11).[43]
4. Both texts mention deliverance from Egypt (Exod 3:7–8; Judg 6:13).
5. Both texts feature the person objecting to the commission (Exod 3:11; Judg 6:15).
6. Both texts promise deliverance from an oppressor through the person (Exod 3:10; Judg 6:16).

---

[40] Hava Shalom-Guy, "The Call Narratives of Gideon and Moses: Literary Convention or More?" *Journal of Hebrew Scriptures* 11 (2011): 13.

[41] The first phrase is quite like those that appear in Gen 26:3; Deut 31:23; Josh 3:7; and Jer 1:8. Shalom-Guy is correct, however, that the "exact phrasing" of the Hebrew phrase occurs only in the calls of Moses and Gideon. Shalom-Guy, 13. The second cluster probably is a stock cluster, since visual perception is a part of the appearances of the angel of Yahweh (cf. Num 22:23, 25, 27, 31; Judg 13:3, 20, 21; 2 Sam 24:17; 1 Chron 21:15, 16; Zech 3:1).

[42] Due to the length of each text, I am dealing only with the immediate context here rather than including the broad context. The immediate context substantiates the point sufficiently.

[43] The third through seventh items in this list come from Miles V. Van Pelt, "Judges," *ESV Expository Commentary* 2 (Crossway, 2021), 574. He also lists the two elements already presented in Shalom-Guy's linguistic evidence and therefore omitted here.

7. Both texts contain confirmatory signs from the Lord (Exod 3:12; Judg 6:17).
8. Both texts possess the narrative order articulated by K. Lawson Younger in these terms: circumstances, authorization, objection, affirmation, sign, and theophany.[44]

These themes provide a strong basis for seeing an intentional allusion in Judges 6 to Exodus 3, a case that would be harder to make based on terms alone. Like the typological patterns described in chapter 1, this allusion shows the correspondence between the saving activity of God in different generations of God's people. When his people are helpless and harassed, the Lord shows his power by selecting weak vessels for immense tasks.[45]

Conclusion

One of fictional detective Harry Bosch's most puzzling cases came when DNA evidence linked a man to a murder that occurred when the man would have been only eight years old.[46] A thorough investigation into the circumstances of the crime presented a different explanation of the DNA. That is what the *themes* instinct offers: confirmatory evidence of what *terms* suggested about the relationship between two texts, or a way to discount the overlap in terms. More is needed, however, to close the case—so let's turn now to the third instinct.

---

[44] K. Lawson Younger, *Judges, Ruth*, rev. ed., NIVAC (Zondervan Academic, 2021), 227.

[45] I think, however, that Jillian Ross is correct that the narrative at the end of Gideon's life (Judg 8:22–27) alludes to Aaron's poor leadership in the golden calf incident (Exod 32:1–6). Jillian L. Ross, *A People Heeds Not Scripture: Allusion in Judges* (Pickwick, 2023), 144–46. The arc in the whole Gideon narrative, then, shows that God gave Israel a new Moses, but this new Moses unfortunately devolved into a new Aaron.

[46] Michael Connelly, *The Drop* (Little, Brown, 2019).

5

Instinct 3: Thesis—Gauge the Allusion's Force

Introduction

Ned was offended. On the first Sunday at the brand-new church plant, Ally gave the welcome and announcements. She wanted attendees to know it was a *come as you are* church, so she pointed out her *Black Panther* T-shirt, head wrap, and jeans. The pastor later told Ally, "Well, I received an angry email about your T-shirt from Ned." Ally was a bit mystified. As a member of the church's launch team, Ned knew the church did not expect formal dress in worship services. She asked, "Why was Ned upset about my shirt?"

"It took me a moment to figure that out," the pastor explained. "He was really upset that we would allow 'that kind of thing' into the church . . . I couldn't understand why a Marvel movie would make someone so upset. Then I realized that he thought your shirt was promoting the Black Panther Party."[1]

---

[1] Ally Henny, *I Won't Shut Up: Finding Your Voice When the World Tries to Silence You* (Baker, 2023), 254–58. Ally is an African American woman, and Ned

What went wrong here?

T-shirts with words or images are *referential* and *communicative*. The words or images refer to something for a purpose. A person's purpose for referring to a film with their T-shirt might be to promote the movie. It might be to create solidarity with other fans of the movie. It might be to communicate that something about the movie describes something about them as fans of the movie. Ally had a communicative purpose for referring to a movie with her T-shirt, but because Ned did not correctly identify the T-shirt's reference, he misinterpreted the purpose of the shirt's communicative referent. When a communicative act refers to something else, you cannot fully interpret that communicative act without grasping its referent.

Can you see the relevance for Old Testament allusions? Like movie T-shirts, Old Testament allusions refer to another text for a purpose. Like Ned, if we don't grasp the purpose of the allusion, we run the risk of misinterpreting (or, more benignly, underappreciating) the purpose of the text as a communicative act. This chapter addresses how to grasp the role an allusion plays in the larger point of an Old Testament text.

Arguing with Allusions

When I was being considered for my current teaching position, the university brought me in for a tour and teaching demonstration. For those who don't know, teaching demonstrations are a form of professional torture whereby a teaching candidate gives a mock lecture to faculty and staff, presumably pretending they are students. There was an underlying purpose to the lecture: convince them I would be a good college professor. Verbal communication involves what philosophers call a **speech act**—that is, the active results sought or accomplished by the use of language—because

---

is a white man. Henny's analysis of the racial implications of the miscommunication are worth reading and pondering.

communicative words seek to accomplish something in the recipient of the speech act.[2] Think about your communication today and ask yourself what you sought to accomplish in the recipient or hearer. If you said at Chick-fil-A, "I'd like a number one, large, with a Coke Zero," you were not merely telling the cashier about your likes and dislikes. Your speech act sought to accomplish the official placing of an order. If they replied, "My pleasure," they were not informing you about their personal passions. Their speech act sought to accomplish in you the feeling of being served well. Written texts, too, are speech acts. They are purposeful "communicative acts" meant to "do specific things" to their audience.[3] Think of the last thing you wrote—what were you trying to do? If you texted your boss, "I will need Saturday off," you sought to accomplish something in your boss's actions. If written communication in general always has a purpose, this is doubly so for Scripture. God says of his communication, "My word that comes from my mouth will not return to me empty, but it will accomplish what I please and will prosper in what I send it to do" (Isa 55:11). God's Word always goes forth to *accomplish* something.

What do speech acts seek to accomplish? Largely, the answer is persuasion. All the communicative examples given so far in this chapter involve some measure of persuasion. The mock lecture, the Chick-fil-A order, and the time-off text all seek to accomplish persuasion. One rhetorical critic explains, "Since before the time of Aristotle, '**rhetoric**' denotes the art of persuasion."[4] George Kennedy offers this definition: "Rhetoric is that quality of discourse by which a speaker or writer seeks to accomplish his purposes."[5] Every speech act—spoken or written—

[2] See Kevin J. Vanhoozer, *Is There a Meaning in This Text?: The Bible, The Reader, and the Morality of Literary Knowledge* (Zondervan, 1998), 428.

[3] Vanhoozer, 228.

[4] Suzanna Smith, "Old Testament Rhetorical and Narrative Criticism," in Mangum and Estes, *Literary Approaches to the Bible*, 79, bold emphasis mine.

[5] George A. Kennedy, *New Testament Interpretation Through Rhetorical Criticism* (University of North Carolina Press, 2014), 3.

involves rhetoric. This is true of the Bible, too, because Scripture is meant to convince sinners to believe in Jesus and then teach, rebuke, correct, and train in following him by his grace (2 Tim 3:15–17). Teaching involves persuasion to the truth; rebuking and correcting involve persuasion away from error or sin; training involves persuasion to a path of formation in grace. Persuasive rhetoric is everywhere in the Bible.

Back to my mock lecture. I really wanted the job, so I turned my speech act's persuasive rhetoric up a notch. I quoted and alluded to a man named John Wesley, the great theologian and founder of Methodism, which was unusual for me. I was not a stranger to Wesley, but as a Reformed-leaning Southern Baptist I felt more at home quoting John Calvin. Why the sudden onslaught of Wesley references? I was applying for a position at a Wesleyan university! The quotes fit the lecture well, and those considering my application knew I was not a native Wesleyan, but I knew that in a room of mostly Wesleyans these references could add two things to my persuasive rhetoric: weight and rapport. Christopher Stanley explains that quotations (and allusions) to another text "are meant to affect an audience; otherwise, there is no reason to include them in a literary work."[6] To *affect* an audience is to persuade them. Stanley lists three ways Paul, for example, sought

---

[6] Christopher D. Stanley, *Arguing with Scripture: The Rhetoric of Quotations in the Letters of Paul* (T&T Clark, 2004), 3. He is speaking here about quotations, but it applies to allusions also. He also thinks, and I agree (this is part of the reason this chapter exists), that the study of the New Testament use of the Old Testament does not give enough attention to "the role of quotations in advancing and sustaining an argument." Stanley, 11–12. He said that in 2004; almost twenty years later, Stanley Porter noted that he thinks this is still an area needing more thought and writing. Stanley Porter, "Rhetoric," *Dictionary of the New Testament Use of the Old Testament* (Baker Academic, 2023), 710. Both Stanley and Porter are talking about the New Testament use of the Old Testament, but since the Old Testament use of the Old Testament is a less-developed field overall, the need for thinking about the rhetorical role of allusions is even greater for the OT.

to *affect* his audience with references to Old Testament texts: (1) to add authority to a claim, (2) to build rapport or commonality with the readers, or (3) to illustrate a point.[7] God could have breathed brand new words in each biblical text, but instead he often chose to embed in several texts references to prior texts. Biblical allusions are a rhetorical, or persuasive, phenomenon.

This persuasive phenomenon is why this chapter's instinct is called *thesis*. Every unit of thought in biblical literature, known as a **pericope** (or distinct passage), has a persuasive point it seeks to affect in the reader. Think of this as the text's *thesis*. We want to know what this thesis is, and in texts where allusions occur, we want to know how that allusion strengthens, enhances, or sharpens the thesis. Remember writing your first five-paragraph essay in school? It all revolved around a thesis: state your thesis in paragraph one, support your thesis in paragraphs two through four, and then restate your thesis in paragraph five. Our teachers wanted us to make sure the material in paragraphs two through four supported the thesis. If we could go back and read our early theses, I'm sure a lot of the material therein did not support our theses. But there is no wasted space in Scripture. The Bible has a thesis to which every book contributes. Every book has a point to which each pericope contributes. Every pericope has a point to which every verse, phrase, and word contributes. Because of the cohesiveness of God's Word, his Spirit enables and helps readers grasp how the parts contribute to the whole. That includes allusions.

This chapter is all about gauging the rhetorical force an allusion adds to a passage. There are two payoffs to this goal. First, it helps confirm that there really is an allusion. Christopher Beetham, writing about the New Testament use of the Old Testament, proposes that one of the essential ingredients to a legitimate allusion is that the alluding

---

[7] Stanley, *Arguing with Scripture*, 13–14.

text cannot be fully understood without understanding the source text.[8] Beetham builds on the work of Richard Hays, who asks two questions in his methodology that are relevant to Beetham's point: "How well does the alleged echo fit into the line of argument that [the writer] is developing?" and "[D]oes the proposed reading make sense?"[9] The sense-making power of grasping an allusion confirms that it isn't a mirage but is a real allusion. Second, gauging the rhetorical force an allusion adds to a passage helps clarify the meaning of the whole passage. If, as Christopher Stanley argued, allusions are purposeful rhetorical acts, then they are integral to the meaning of the passage employing them. Returning to the chapter's opening example, Ned did not understand Ally's choice of T-shirt until he identified and learned its actual referent.

Questions for Gauging the Force of a Proposed Allusion

The twenty-first century is a great time to be a DIYer, mostly on account of YouTube. Needing new brake pads presented me with my first DIY, money-saving opportunity because my buddy Scott assured me a novice could learn. I learned quickly that the job would be much easier with a little specialized tool called a brake pad spreader. You can change brake pads without it, but it helps to use this specialized tool. The task at hand in this chapter is to detect the thesis, or rhetorical force, of a passage and then determine whether a proposed allusion enhances the thesis or not. Just like there is a tool for changing brake pads, there is a specific tool for

[8] Christopher A. Beetham, *Echoes of Scripture in the Letter of Paul to the Colossians*, BibInt 96 (Brill, 2008), 30.

[9] These are numbers four and seven in his classic seven-part approach to the New Testament use of the Old Testament (what he calls "echoes"). Richard B. Hays, *Echoes of Scripture in the Letters of Paul* (Yale University Press, 1989), 29–32.

detecting the rhetorical thesis of a passage known as **rhetorical criticism**, or **rhetorical analysis**. George Kennedy defines the enterprise like this: "The ultimate goal of rhetorical analysis, briefly put, is the discovery of the author's intent and of how that is transmitted through a text to an audience."[10] I argue elsewhere that when studying Old Testament allusions, scholars sometimes mention the issue of rhetoric but do not use the tool of rhetorical criticism.[11] This chapter seeks to correct that and aims to discover how an alluding text's use of a source text serves the alluding author's persuasive goals for their audience.[12] This discovery is guided by four questions:[13]

1. How is the text arranged, and where does the allusion fit?
2. What general human situation or spiritual condition does the text address?
3. What is the alluding text's persuasive goal for the situation it addresses?
4. How does the source text assist the alluding text in its persuasive goal?

Now let's walk through the rationale for each question and some examples for how this uncovers the *thesis* an allusion serves.

---

[10] Kennedy, *New Testament Interpretation*, 12.

[11] Matthew E. Swale, *From Recollection to Recommitment: The Rhetorical Function of Allusions to Judges in Psalms 68, 83, and 106*, BBR Dissertation Series 1 (Gorgias, 2024), 6n14.

[12] Swale, 3.

[13] The first three questions are adapted from George Kennedy's New Testament methodology and the way that two Old Testament scholars adapt it to Old Testament studies. Kennedy, *New Testament Interpretation*, 32–27; Ryan J. Cook, "Prayers That Form Us: Rhetoric and Psalms Interpretation," *JSOT* 39, no. 4 (2015): 458; Karl Möller, *A Prophet in Debate: The Rhetoric of Persuasion in the Book of Amos*, JSOTSS (Sheffield Academic, 2003), 37–43.

1) How is the text arranged, and where does the allusion fit?

There are TV shows you can pop into for an episode here or there without missing an overarching storyline (e.g., *Bones*), and there are shows that need to be viewed from episode one to the series finale to be fully grasped (e.g., *Parenthood*). In the latter type, each episode has its own self-contained beginning, end, flow, and goal that contributes to a bigger narrative. Each pericope in biblical literature is like one of those episodes: possessing a self-contained beginning, end, flow, and goal that contributes to the rhetoric of its overall biblical book.[14]

Finding the beginning and end of a pericope and tracking its structure are both standard features of biblical exegesis.[15] Rhetorical analysis prizes these features because each pericope's rhetorical goal unfolds in a purposeful way. The placement of the allusion should be noted because it plays a strategic role in the text's unfolding rhetorical purpose. First Samuel 8 is a great example of this. Sometimes chapter divisions do not isolate the beginning and end of a pericope, but the divisions do a good job in 1 Samuel 8. Verse 1 introduces a new chronological setting compared to the end of chapter 7, and verse 22 ends with a measure of closure before chapter 9 introduces a new character. So, in 1–2 Samuel, chapter 8 is its own pericope. The structure of the narrative, after introducing the setting, unfolds through a dialogue between Israel's elders and Samuel, Samuel and the Lord, and then the elders and Samuel again. The structure can be visualized like this:

I. Israel's Political Setting: Samuel's Failed Successors (1 Sam 8:1–3)
II. Israel's Political Request: A King Like the Nations (vv. 4–5)

---

[14] A growing body of literature argues for a discernible flow even in books like Psalms and Proverbs. For introductions, see O. Palmer Robertson, *The Flow of the Psalms: Discovering Their Structure and Theology* (P&R, 2015); Ryan P. O'Dowd, *Proverbs*, The Story of God Bible Commentary (Zondervan, 2017), 29–31.

[15] Douglas Stuart, *Old Testament Exegesis: A Handbook for Students and Pastors*, 4th ed. (WJK, 2009), 5, 15.

III. Israel's Political Idolatry: Rejecting Yahweh's Kingship (vv. 6–9)
IV. Israel's Political Warning: A King Who Takes (vv. 10–18)
V. Israel's Political Insistence: A King Like the Nations (vv. 19–22)

The author alludes to two Old Testament texts in three places in this passage, and their locations in the passage are strategic.

First, verse 3 says that Samuel's sons—his chosen successors—"turned toward dishonest profit, took bribes [*šōḥad*], and perverted [*nāṭâ*] justice." The terms *šōḥad* and *nāṭâ* only occur together in three verses: the present text, Prov 17:23, and Deut 16:19.[16] First Samuel 8:3 and Deut 16:19 have something in common that makes Deuteronomy the more likely source text here: they both talk about the leadership office of judges. Deuteronomy 16:19 says that judges and officials must not do three things: "deny [*nāṭâ*] justice," "show partiality," or "accept a bribe [*šōḥad*]." So, the narrator in 1 Samuel 8 wants readers to know at the outset that Israel was suffering from leadership that deliberately disobeyed Mosaic leadership regulations. Putting this allusion in the introductory setting section, common in biblical narratives, sets the tone for measuring leadership against the backdrop of Deuteronomy throughout the story.

Second, verses 5 and 20 both use the phrase *like* (*k-*) *all* (*kōl*) *the nations* (*gôy*). This exact phrase in Hebrew occurs only in 1 Sam 8:5, 20; Ezek 25:8; and Deut 17:14. Deuteronomy 17:14 is the most likely source text because it also shares an additional phrase with 1 Sam 8:5 that is not in 1 Sam 8:20: *appoint* (*śûm*) *a king* (*melek̠*).[17] First Samuel 8:5 reports the Israelite elders' request for a king, and 8:20 restates the request after Yahweh's word of rebuke (vv. 6–9) and warning (vv. 10–18) came through

[16] All three texts also use the standard word for *justice* or *judgment*, *mišpāṭ*.

[17] Also, Ezek 25:8 is voiced by non-Israelite nations about Israel, whereas in 1 Samuel 8 and Deuteronomy 17 are both spoken by Israelites desiring a king. The total combination of "all" (*kōl*), "nation" (*gôy*), "appoint" (*śûm*), and "king" (*melek̠*) also occurs in Jer 25:9, but in the context of a non-Israelite king used as a vessel of God's judgment.

Samuel. The elders' words allude to Deut 17:14–20, where Moses predicts the Israelites would want a king like the nations and then lays down six rules to make Israelite kings *unlike* the nations. Schnittjer summarizes well the import of the allusion: "The narrative identifies the motivation of the people to be at odds with the will of Yahweh regarding the law of the king."[18] Why does it matter where the two allusions (1 Sam 8:5, 20) occur in the structure of the story? The requests come before and after the Lord speaks to (vv. 6–9) and through (vv. 10–18) Samuel about the elders' idolatrous and shortsighted request. So, the placement of three allusions to two Deuteronomy texts show that in the context of judges who disobeyed Deuteronomy (vv. 1–3), the elders of Israel also disobeyed Deuteronomy (v. 5) and then doubled down on their disobedience to Deuteronomy (v. 20) after hearing God's perspective on the matter (vv. 6–18). By including the second allusion to Deut 17:14 in verse 20, the author highlights the recalcitrance of the anti-Deuteronomic spiritual climate already introduced in verse 3's allusion. The writer communicates this not only by the *presence* of allusions, but also by their *placement*.

2) What general human situation or spiritual condition does the text address?

The note read, "I want it to end." When fictional detective Will Trent heard that the body of a deceased young lady was found with this note, he was not convinced it was a suicide. By the end of the episode of *Will Trent*, Will and his partner Faith discover the note's "it" was not a reference to the woman's life but to a drug pilfering scheme she was being pressured by her university research lab to maintain. She wanted her involvement in illegal activity to end. The note addressed a particular situation, and properly interpreting the crime scene was not possible until that situation

[18] Gary Edward Schnittjer, *Old Testament Use: A Book-by-Book Guide* (Zondervan, 2021), 179.

was identified.[19] Likewise, biblical interpretation is sharpened when the situation being addressed is considered.

Rhetorical critics call this the *rhetorical situation*, or the reason the rhetorical event of the text came to be.[20] For some Old Testament texts, like Haggai, the rhetorical situation can be identified. For some Old Testament texts, like Psalm 1 or other anonymous psalms, the rhetorical situation is more difficult to identify. This is common especially in the Psalms, probably because many of them are intentionally vague about their specific situation so that subsequent worshipers could readily sing and pray them.[21] Ryan Cook adapted the concept of a rhetorical situation to Psalms studies by simply asking what "human problem or condition (within an ancient Near Eastern context) . . . the psalm is attempting to address."[22]

Bryan Chapell argues persuasively that the fallen condition of humanity is addressed by every passage of Scripture,[23] so it seems Cook's proposal is useful for rhetorical analysis outside of the Psalms too. Because my students struggled with the concept of a rhetorical situation, I found it helpful to use Chapell's concept of a passage's Fallen Condition Focus (FCF) to get at the concept of passage's aiming their rhetoric at a situation or need. Chapell defines a passage's FCF as "the mutual human condition that contemporary persons share with those to or about whom the text was written that required the grace of the passage for God's people to glorify and enjoy him."[24] Chapell explains that while often the FCF is a sin issue like greed or idolatry, sometimes the FCF is not a sin issue but an issue of being fallen, finite people in a broken world—grief or bodily

---

19 *Will Trent*, season 2, episode 8, "Two Hundred Dollars and a Bus Pass," aired February 8, 2023.

20 Kennedy, *New Testament Interpretation*, 34.

21 James L. Mays, *Psalms*, Interpretation (WJK, 1994), 23.

22 Cook, "Prayers That Form Us," 457.

23 Bryan Chapell, *Christ-Centered Preaching: Redeeming the Expository Sermon*, 3rd ed. (Baker Academic, 2018), 29.

24 Chapell, 30.

frailty, for example.[25] Chapell roots the concept in 2 Tim 3:16–17, "All Scripture is inspired by God and is profitable for teaching, for rebuking, for correcting, for training in righteousness, so that the man of God may be *complete*, equipped for every good work" (italics added). Why would God's Word *complete* a redeemed man or woman of God? Because "we are incomplete," and each biblical text addresses "our lack of wholeness" with God's restorative grace.[26] The Ten Commandments are perhaps the easiest texts for identifying the FCF. What human need necessitated the command not to covet (Exod 20:17)? The fallen human tendency toward ingratitude and the idolatry of possessions. Other texts might be harder to identify. What human need necessitated the command to praise in Ps 117:1–2? The fallen human tendency to *not* glorify God, or the tendency for worshipers to become complacent or perfunctory in worshiping God.[27]

A text's FCF is like the spiritual target at which the text aims its rhetorical arrow. Here are two examples of how to identify an alluding text's FCF with a view toward understanding the rhetorical purpose of its allusion. First, Hag 1:1–11 relays the Lord's rebuke to the postexilic people of God for building their own homes but not rebuilding the temple (v. 4). The FCF, then, would relate to the fallen human tendency to prioritize comfort over covenantal commitments to corporate worship. How brilliant, then, for Hag 1:4 to refer to the returners' homes as "paneled" (*sāp̄an*). Three of six total uses of *sāp̄an* occur in descriptions of Solomon building the temple (1 Kgs 6:15) and his lavish palace (7:3, 7). Schnittjer explains

---

[25] Chapell, 32.

[26] Chapell, 30.

[27] Calls to praise in the Psalms (e.g., 99:1; 117:1; 145:1) are great examples of texts whose FCF need not be a sin issue, but a frailty or finitude issue. Davida Charney explains that praise rhetoric in the Psalms can function as "regular maintenance work" because "even at the best of times, Israelite speakers are well aware of the precariousness of their paths and the need to use praise activity to maintain their balance." Davida Charney, *Persuading God: Rhetorical Studies of First-Person Psalms*, Hebrew Bible Monographs 73 (Sheffield Phoenix, 2017), 18–20.

that through this allusion, "Haggai accuses the people of living in temple-like houses while the temple remains in ruins."[28] Because the writer of 1–2 Kings raises questions about Solomon's priorities by pointing out that he spent nearly double the time on constructing his palace than he did on the temple (1 Kgs 6:38–7:1),[29] Haggai's allusion to Solomon's construction endeavors may also highlight their unfaithful priorities.

Second, Proverbs 3 presents fatherly instruction to pursue covenantally faithful wisdom. This section's FCF relates to the fallen human tendency toward foolish self-reliance (vv. 5, 7) because it is easier than submitting to divine discipline to gain wisdom (vv. 11–12). This fallen tendency is the spiritual target at which Proverbs 3 is aimed, and two allusions help the arrow hit the target. One is when Prov 3:3 urges wisdom by pairing the verbs *tie* (*qāšar*) and *write* (*kāṯaḇ*), the writer alludes to the way Moses challenged Israel to *bind* (*qāšar*) and *write* (*kāṯaḇ*) the commands of Deuteronomy to home and heart (6:8–9; 11:18–20). The other allusion comes in Prov 3:18 with the phrase "tree [*ʿēṣ*] of life [*ḥay*]." The phrase only occurs in Genesis 2–3 and in Proverbs (3:18; 11:30; 13:12; 15:4), where it functions as a metaphor for flourishing with God in an Edenic manner once barred from sinners (Gen 3:24). The combined effect of the two allusions addresses the FCF powerfully by relating the pursuit of wisdom with what was lost in Eden and what was commanded by Moses.[30]

3) What is the alluding text's persuasive goal for the situation it addresses?

Over the years, my wife and I watched many of the Marvel films as they released. As I write, we are rewatching our favorites with our oldest son and

---

[28] Schnittjer, *Old Testament Use*, 439.

[29] Paul R. House, *1, 2 Kings*, NAC 8 (B&H, 1995), 130.

[30] Christopher B. Ansberry, "Book of Proverbs," *Dictionary of the New Testament Use of the Old Testament* (Baker Academic, 2023), 649–50.

our daughter. I had forgotten that Ant-Man first grows to several stories tall in *Captain America: Civil War*. Ant-Man possesses three categories of physical makeup, and each has its own general goal. Regular-sized Ant-Man's goal, I suppose, is to live a regular life. Ant-sized Ant-Man's goal is to sneak up on opponents in combat or to go places that are otherwise inaccessible. Giant-sized Ant-Man's goal is to present a larger fighting presence in battle scenes (at least that's the case in *Captain America: Civil War*). Classically, rhetoric has been understood to possess three categories with specific goals. First, there is *judicial rhetoric*. Its goal is "to persuade the audience to make a judgment about events occurring in the past."[31] Second, *epideictic rhetoric* wants to move the audience "to hold or reaffirm some point of view in the present."[32] Third, *deliberative rhetoric* has as its goal "to persuade" the audience "to take some action in the future."[33] Judicial looks to the past, epideictic to the present, and deliberative to the future.

These categories may seem artificial, but they map nicely onto the three main goals Scripture possesses for its readers. They are everywhere in the Bible, but the Lord Jesus commences his ministry by stating all three: "*Repent* and *believe* the good news!" and then a few verses later, "*Follow* me" (Mark 1:15b, 17, italics added). Repent, believe, follow.[34] Repentance, like judicial rhetoric, looks to the past by pointing out sinful or idolatrous patterns. Belief, like epideictic rhetoric, involves trust in the present (even if present trust is in future promises). Obedience, like deliberative rhetoric, looks toward future action or way of life. So, even

---

[31] Kennedy, *New Testament Interpretation*, 19.

[32] Kennedy, 19.

[33] Kennedy, 19.

[34] For these three primary applicational goals of Scripture, I am indebted to my former pastor in Birmingham, Alabama: Dr. Bob Flayhart. He articulates the third step with the rhetorically powerful word *fight* (i.e., repent, believe, fight). He calls these three steps "The Gospel Waltz" because of their continuous nature. See Bob Flayhart and Holly Mackle, *The Gospel Waltz: Experiencing the Transformational Power of Grace* (GCD Books, 2023).

though Old Testament authors urge repentance, faith, and obedience in countless ways, these are their broad rhetorical goals. To make sure you are reading the rhetorical goals of the alluding text well, it is wise to consult scholarly works like commentaries to see how they describe its persuasive thrust.

Hosea's allusions to Scripture demonstrate how these three goals play out in Old Testament allusions. First, Hos 9:9 urges repentance by comparing the past sins of the northern kingdom of Israel with the most egregious sins in Israel's history: "They have deeply corrupted themselves / as in the days of Gibeah. He will remember their iniquity; / he will punish their sins." The "days of Gibeah" look back to a text discussed in this book already, Judges 19,[35] because its atrocities occurred in Gibeah. The past orientation is even clearer in Hos 10:9a: "Israel, you have sinned / since the days of Gibeah." Hosea seeks to persuade them of their egregious history of covenant breaking by placing it in continuity with Judges 19. Second, Hos 11:8 urges belief that Yahweh will restore Israel after judgment when he says, "How can I give you up, Ephraim? / How can I surrender you, Israel? / How can I make you like Admah? / How can I treat you like Zeboiim? / I have had a change of heart; / my compassion is stirred!" Admah and Zeboiim were part of the motley crew of judged cities headlined by Sodom and Gomorrah (Deut 29:23).[36] Though Israel behaved like Sodom (9:9), Yahweh will not treat them as he did Sodom (11:8). This is good news that, for Hosea's believing readers, would invite faith and hope. Third, Hos 12:3 urges obedience by alluding to how Jacob wrestled with God (see chapter 3). I think Luther was correct that Hosea's use of Genesis 32 is "imitative"; in other words, Hosea is trying to goad covenant fidelity: instead of striving to maintain idol worship, strive to worshipfully

---

[35] Derek D. Bass, "Hosea's Use of Scripture: An Analysis of His Hermeneutics," (PhD diss., Southern Baptist Theological Seminary, 2008), 203.

[36] Bass explains how the allusion is both to the introduction of these cities in Genesis 14 and to the judgment narrative in Genesis 19. Bass, 221–24.

interact with Yahweh.[37] In various and sundry ways, Hosea—like other biblical authors—uses prior Scripture to persuade readers to repentance, faith, and obedience.

4) How does the source text assist the alluding text in its persuasive goal?

Here's the payoff. The previous three questions uncover the *thesis* of the alluding text, and this question explores whether the proposed allusion contributes to the *thesis*. I've read a few high school and college essays over the years, and not everything students include in their essay contributes to the thesis (if there is a discernible thesis). Thanks to the superintending work of the Holy Spirit, however, biblical writers do not include anything that does not contribute to the overall goal of each biblical text and book. So, if the allusion is genuine, synergy will exist between the rhetorical force of the alluding text and the source text. The source text will intensify the alluding text's rhetorical force.

For example, let's return to chapter 4's claim that both *terms* and *themes* evince an allusion to Gen 3:16 in Song 7:10. What would Gen 3:16 contribute to the persuasive goal of Song 7:10? At least three things (that seismically shifted my understanding of Song of Songs). First, the allusion adds to Song 6:4–8:4 a claim bubbling beneath the surface of Song of Songs with every use of the word *garden* (*gan*): something lost in Eden is being restored. Ellen Davis writes that the relational and marital "distortion" introduced in Gen 3:16 "is now corrected; the original symmetry that obtained between woman and man is restored."[38] Among the bridegroom and bride of the Song, something Edenic is being reclaimed. If that was all Solomon wanted to convey in Song 7:10, he could have

[37] Martin Luther, *Lectures on Genesis Chapters 31–37*, Luther's Works 6 (Concordia, 1970), 126.

[38] Ellen F. Davis, *Proverbs, Ecclesiastes, and the Song of Songs*, Westminster Bible Companion (WJK, 2000), 294.

alluded to, say, Gen 2:25, "Both the man and his wife were naked, yet felt no shame." Instead, Solomon alluded to a text adjacent to the famed messianic promise in Gen 3:15. After all, it is not marriage *itself* that brings Edenic restoration but what marriage foreshadows (Eph 5:31–32).

So, second, the allusion adds that Song 6:4–8:4 foreshadows a greater restoration than only restoring Edenic marital intimacy. Marital harmony was disrupted (Gen 3:16) because sin disrupted human harmony with God (4:7).[39] Alluding to Gen 3:16 does more than evoke *one* element of Eden restored. Sin disrupted intrahuman relationship, but also divine-human relationship and even humanity's relationship with creation.[40] James Hamilton argues the allusion in Song 7:10 "indicates that the reconciliation here will be *as far reaching as the curse has been*."[41] Solomon casts marital bliss as a foretaste of the eschatological bliss to come through his royal descendant.[42] This allusion changed the way I read Song of Songs.[43]

---

[39] Recall that *tᵊšûqâ* is only used in Song 7:10; Gen 3:16; 4:7. Although I think the allusion is primarily to Gen 3:16, it is likely that the author means to also allude to Gen 4:7.

[40] Davis, *Proverbs*, 232.

[41] James M. Hamilton Jr., *Song of Songs: A Biblical-Theological, Allegorical, Christological Interpretation* (Christian Focus, 2015), 131. Italics original.

[42] Christopher W. Mitchell, *The Song of Songs*, Concordia Commentary (Concordia, 2003), 1111–13; David is widely recognized in evangelical biblical theology as a unique type of Christ, but Solomon should be thought of in this way also. Given the role of Solomon in the promises of 2 Samuel 7, this makes sense. Solomon's messianic import clicked for me when I realized that Song of Songs' psalm-style superscription in 1:1b, "Solomon's" (*lišᵊlōmô*, i.e., the preposition *l-* prefixed to Solomon's name), only occurs as a superscription elsewhere in Psalm 72 and Psalm 127. Both of these psalms ooze with messianic hope. The messianic hope in Psalm 72 is widely recognized, though in Psalm 127 it is often overlooked. For Solomon, "house" (127:1) and "offspring" (127:3) were the key ingredients of his role in the Davidic covenant promises (2 Sam 7:12–13). See O. Palmer Robertson, *The Flow of the Psalms: Discovering Their Structure and Theology* (P&R, 2015), 213–14.

[43] Most Bible students will be aware of what Douglas O'Donnell articulates, "The first major challenge is to determine whether the Song is an

Ruling Out a Proposed Allusion Because of an Unconvincing Thesis

Chapter 2 included a quip from my favorite fictional lawyer: "A trial often comes down to who is a better storyteller, the prosecution or the defense. There is evidence, of course, but physical evidence is at first interpreted for the jury by the storyteller."[44] Without a sense-making story, evidence falls flat. If the proposed allusion does not make sense within the pericope's broader rhetorical story, the terms and themes in common may be coincidental instead of intentional. I think this is the case in the example of Psalm 110 and Judges 6–8.

Raymond Tournay argues that Psalm 110 alludes to the Gideon narrative (Judges 6–8).[45] The terms and themes involved support his argument. The passages share four terms illustrated in the chart:[46]

---

allegory about God's love for his people or an erotic poem about human love set in the context of marriage." Douglas S. O'Donnell, "The Song of Solomon," in *ESV Expository Commentary: Psalms-Song of Solomon*, ESV Expository Commentary 5 (Crossway, 2022), 1123. Most are probably also aware that modern commentators usually opt for the second of O'Donnell's options. Allusions have convinced me that James Hamilton is correct when he argues that the book is about both marriage and the gospel. Hamilton, *Song of Songs*, 28–33. I began to be open to what these allusions might imply about the book as a whole because of the work of my brother (e.g., Ryan Swale, "Delighting in the Love of the Bridegroom: The Song of Songs in Seventeenth-Century Scottish Spirituality," *Puritan Reformed Journal* 17, no. 1 [2025]: 59–76).

[44] Michael Connelly, *The Law of Innocence* (Little, Brown, 2020), 190.

[45] Raymond J. Tournay, "Les Relectures Du Psaume 110 (109) et l'allusion à Gédéon," *RB* 105, no. 2 (1998): 326–31. The only other scholar I have come across who might agree is Geoffrey Grogan, who calls these proposed connections "possible allusions." Geoffrey W. Grogan, *Psalms*, THOTC (Eerdmans, 2008), 184.

[46] Tournay mentions *dew*, *send*, and *head*, but I have added the others to steel man his argument.

Psalm 110 ALLUDING TEXT	Selections from Judges 6 SOURCE TEXT
This is the declaration of the LORD to my Lord: "Sit at my right hand until I make your enemies your footstool." The LORD will extend [*šālaḥ*] your mighty scepter from Zion. Rule over your surrounding enemies. Your people will volunteer on your day of battle [*ḥayil*]. In holy splendor, from the womb of the dawn, the dew [*ṭal*] of your youth belongs to you. The LORD has sworn an oath and will not take it back: "You are a priest forever according to the pattern of Melchizedek." The Lord is at your right hand; he will crush kings on the day of his anger. He will judge the nations, heaping up corpses; he will crush leaders [*rōʾš*] over the entire world. He will drink from the brook by the road; therefore, he will lift up his head [*rōʾš*].[47]	And the angel of the LORD appeared to him and said to him, "The LORD is with you, O mighty man of valor [*ḥayil*]" (Judg 6:12 ESV). The LORD turned to him and said, "Go in the strength you have and deliver Israel from the grasp of Midian. I am sending [*šālaḥ*] you!" (v. 14). And build an altar to the LORD your God on the top [*rōʾš*] of the stronghold here (v. 26a ESV).[48] That night God did as Gideon requested: only the fleece was dry, and dew [*ṭal*] was all over the ground (v. 40).

[47] Psalm 110:7 uses a different word for *lift* or *raise*, but this is a similar idiom to the one in Judg 8:28a, "So Midian was subdued before the people of Israel, and they raised their heads no more" (ESV). This is something of an overlap in *terms* and *themes*.

[48] This is a different meaning for *rōʾš* than in Psalm 110, because the word can refer to a human head, an animal's head, hair on one's head, a person, the top

"Dew" (*tal*) only occurs thirty-one times in the Old Testament, but the rest of the terms each occur hundreds of times. As far as *themes* go, Tournay points out two. First, both Psalm 110 and the wider Gideon narrative involve mass death (Judg 8:10; Ps 110:6). Second, both Psalm 110 and the wider Gideon narrative contain instances of drinking on the go (Judg 7:7; Ps 110:7).[49]

What would be the alluding text's *thesis*, and how would alluding to Gideon serve that rhetorical point? Tournay argues that the psalmist is casting the coming Davidic ruler as being characterized by a Gideon-like vigor and focus in battle.[50] It is not clear, however, that vigor and focus characterize Gideon. Richard Nelson argues that until Judg 7:15—well after the term "dew" (6:36–40) and the drinking episode (7:1–6)—Gideon is characterized as an "insecure doubter" rather than a laser-focused commando.[51] Once he moves past his insecurity, he acts heroically (vv. 15–25) but then mercilessly humiliates and kills his own countrymen (8:16–17) before leading Israel back into idol worship (vv. 24–35). Because the final word on Gideon is ambiguous at best and negative at worst,[52] it is

---

of something, the beginning of something, something that is the best, a leader, a military unit, or a numeric value. *HALOT*, 1164–67.

[49] Tournay, "Psaume 110," 329–30. Tournay also capitalizes on a connection outside of Psalm 110 to make his argument. Isaiah 9 predicts a Davidic ruler (v. 7) winning a victory like that "on the day of Midian" (v. 4). The idea is that if Isaiah 9 connects the victories of Gideon and the coming Davidic king, Psalm 110 might also. I would argue that by not mentioning Gideon by name in Isaiah 9, the focus is on God's heroic intervention in the face of Israel's spiritual darkness (Isa 9:1–2) rather than on Gideon himself.

[50] Tournay, 330.

[51] Richard D. Nelson, *Judges: A Critical & Rhetorical Commentary* (Bloomsbury, 2017), 152.

[52] Daniel Block offers sixteen elements of the Gideon narrative that challenge a heroic interpretation of Gideon and promote the bookwide portrayal of both Israel and her leaders in "increasing and intensifying spiritual and social degradation." Daniel I. Block, "Will the Real Gideon Please Stand Up?: Narrative Style and Intention in Judges 6–9," *JETS* 40, no. 3 (September 1997), 359–62, 365.

difficult to see how a psalm meant to inspire hope in a coming priest-king is helped rhetorically by alluding to Gideon.[53]

Given the Davidic superscription, it would make more rhetorical sense for the psalmist to intend a comparison between the priest-king and David the warrior than Gideon. Indeed, all the terms the psalm shares with the Gideon narrative are also found in various Davidic narratives.[54] In other words, David's battle résumé bolsters the rhetoric of Psalm 110 more self-evidently than Gideon's. Without thinking of the alluding text's *thesis* and what a proposed allusion contributes to it, Tournay's proposed allusion would be far more convincing.

Confirming a Proposed Allusion Because of a Convincing Thesis

What about potential allusions that lean heavily on the allusion's rhetorical explanatory power? Russell Meek provides an exciting example of this scenario by arguing that a famous keyword in Ecclesiastes—*futility* (*hebel*)—alludes to the first murder victim in the Bible,[55] Abel (Gen 4:1–16). It may surprise readers of the English text to hear that the Hebrew spelling of *hebel* is identical to that of the Hebrew proper

[53] Erhard Gerstenberger is probably right when he explains the rhetorical intention of Psalm 110 like this: "The focus on the divine savior of the faithful, acting both politically and spiritually, after the battle and final victory, envisions an ultimate, urgently longed-for rehabilitation of the community." Erhard S. Gerstenberger, *Psalms, Part 2, and Lamentations*, FOTL 15 (Eerdmans, 2001), 267.

[54] For example, *šālaḥ* (114x in 1 Samuel 16–2 Samuel 24), *ḥayil* (17x in 1 Samuel 16–2 Samuel 24), *ṭal* (2 Sam 1:21; 17:12), *rōʾš* (43x in 1 Samuel 16–2 Samuel 24). The word for *river* in Ps 110:7 (*naḥal*) also occurs 9x in Davidic narratives (1 Samuel 16–2 Samuel 24) but not the Gideon narrative.

[55] The translation range conveys the complexity of the Hebrew word, e.g., "vanity" (KJV, RSV, ESV), "pointless" (CJB), "futile" (CSB, NET), "meaningless" (NIV), "useless" (NCV), and "vapor" (EHV).

noun Abel.[56] The allusion, then, is sprinkled throughout the thirty-eight uses of *hebel* in Ecclesiastes. Meek admits the proposal is "far from a slam dunk case. It's only one Hebrew word, and the thematic overlap requires some biblical-theological maneuvering with which some [scholars] take issue."[57]

Meek offers three reasons the allusion should be considered, and the third relates to the text's rhetorical *thesis*. First, the allusion is on brand because Ecclesiastes often alludes to Genesis.[58] Second, *hebel* (literally, "vapor") refers metaphorically either to "things that do not last" (e.g., human life or wealth) or "things that do not produce their intended results" (e.g., idolatry or vain speech). The life of Abel illustrates both of these broad metaphors:[59] Abel's life was brief like a vapor, and Abel's righteous life did not produce the expected earthly blessings (i.e., the retribution principle in the OT).[60] Third, relevant to the *thesis* instinct, Meek explains that alluding to Abel allows the writer of Ecclesiastes to walk a fine rhetorical line between the goodness of living faithfully like Abel (e.g., Eccl 12:13–14) and the "vagaries of life" like Abel experienced

---

[56] If you use one of the tools recommended in chapter 2 or a standard Hebrew lexicon, they will be different numbered entries of the same Hebrew word, (i.e., *hebel*-I and *hebel*-II), but the root and spelling are identical.

[57] Russell L. Meek, *Ecclesiastes and the Search for Meaning in an Upside-Down World* (Hendrickson, 2022), 31.

[58] Meek, 49. Meek argues for allusions in Eccl 2:4–6 (to Gen 2:2, 8–10), 3:11 (to Genesis 1, broadly), 3:18–21 (to Gen 3:7; 19), 12:7 (to Gen 2:7; 3:19), seven passages (Eccl 2:24–26; 3:10–15, 16–22; 5:18–20; 8:10–15; 9:7–10; 11:8–10) using themes from Gen 2:15–25, and two passages (Eccl 8:11; 9:3) employing themes from Gen 6:5; 8:21. Meek, 1–27. Although he does not see all the allusions Meek does (only treating the allusion in Eccl 12:7 to Gen 2:7; 3:19–21), Schnittjer summarizes the field like this: "Many suggest Ecclesiastes relies on themes of Gen 1–11." Schnittjer, *Old Testament Use*, 601.

[59] Meek, *Ecclesiastes*, 33–37. Meek does not argue that Abel relates to each specific connotation (i.e., idolatry or wealth) but to the two broad categories of metaphorical meaning.

[60] Meek, 45, 49.

(e.g., Gen 4:8; Eccl 8:14).[61] For Meeks, the rhetorical contribution of an Abel allusion to the *thesis* of Ecclesiastes makes it a convincing proposal.

Conclusion

The first time I remember noticing an Easter Egg in a Disney movie was when a figurine that looked like the Beast from *Beauty and the Beast* showed up among the sultan's figurines in *Aladdin*.[62] If the term "Easter Egg" is new to you, it is the nickname fans have given to semihidden references in one movie to another movie. Disney's Easter Eggs are *almost* like Old Testament allusions. As far as I can tell, seeing the Beast in *Aladdin* adds nothing to the plot other than a little fun if you notice the reference. I don't know of a compelling theory linking the two narrative worlds. Old Testament allusions are different: they assist the rhetorical force of the alluding passage integrally. In this way, they are more like the Easter Eggs in the Marvel Cinematic Universe (MCU) that demonstrate the ways each film contributes to the overarching storyline of Marvel's integrally connected films. Comparing biblical allusions to Marvel's Easter Eggs, Benjamin Gladd writes, "Easter eggs are the tissue that binds each Marvel movie to the MCU's larger story."[63] Viewers miss something about the filmmakers' *thesis* if they miss the Easter Eggs—so with the Holy Spirit as our guide, let's seek to grow in apprehending the author-intended "Easter Eggs" throughout the Old Testament and the *theses* they assist.

---

[61] Meek, 50.

[62] *Aladdin*, directed by Ron Clements and John Musker (Walt Disney Pictures, 1992).

[63] Benjamin L. Gladd, "Keep Watch for Biblical Allusions," The Carson Center, July 25, 2024, https://www.thegospelcoalition.org/article/watch-biblical-allusions/. Gladd's article deals with NT allusions to the OT.

6

Practicing the Instincts: Psalm 145 as a Case Study

Introduction

If there is a Disney character I want to be like when I grow up, it's Smokey from *Cars 3*. When Lightning McQueen lacks direction for life and career but cannot turn to his deceased mentor, Doc Hudson, he meets Doc's old friend Smokey. While the rest of the world uses high-tech training methods, Smokey imparts forgotten racing instincts through unconventional experiences. Dodging hay bales, maneuvering through a herd of cows, and driving through a forest at night without headlights didn't make sense until the final race. Then, Smokey's methods provided the instincts to "sneak through the window" between racers and compete with dexterity. The instincts made sense in action.[1] The goal of this chapter is to get out on the interpretive track and show the three instincts in action, first in an extended form and then in an abbreviated worksheet

[1] *Cars 3*, directed by Brian Fee (Pixar Animation Studios, 2017).

that might be more appropriate for sermon preparation or a brief academic assignment. This chapter will explore the proposal that Ps 145:18 alludes to Deut 4:7.

As is often the case, this chapter's proposal started with a hunch. It seemed like Ps 145:18 was talking about doing the very thing Deut 4:7 said Israel ought to do as a nation. As I investigated the hunch and have continued to do so, I have not encountered anyone else who thinks Ps 145:18 alludes to Deut 4:7.[2] Sometimes biblical studies literature does not confirm a hunch because the hunch is misguided.[3] One must always be open to that possibility. But sometimes no one has written about the hunch because the Bible's riches are bottomless, and the scholarly literature on the Old Testament use of the Old Testament is young. When it comes to identifying Old Testament allusions, there are many unturned stones.

---

[2] A survey of forty-six Psalms commentaries indicated that no one has proposed this (L. Allen, Alter, Augustine, Broyles, Berlin [with Shinan and Sommer], Bullock, Brueggemann, Brueggemann and Bellinger, Calvin, Cassiodorus, Clifford, Collins, deClaisse-Walford [NICOT], Dahood, Eaton, Ester, Futato, Gerstenberger, Goldingay, Hamilton, Harman, Hossfeld and Zenger, Keil and Delitzsch, Kidner, Kraus, Leupold, Longman, Mays, McCann, Murphy, Perowne, Rhodes, Rogerson and McKay, Ross, Schaefer, Terrien, Theodoret of Cyrus, VanGemeren, Waltner, Webster, Weiser, Wilcock), though there is the possibility that the proposal exists somewhere. These commentators acknowledge the two texts as cross-references without claiming that one depends on the other intentionally: A. A. Anderson, *The Book of Psalms*, vol. 2, repr., NCBC (Eerdmans, 1989), 939; John Bradford, "Only Christ Brings Our Requests to God," *Psalms 73–150*, RCOS 8, ed. Herman J. Selderhuis (InterVarsity, 2018), 378; Geoffrey Grogan, *Psalms*, THOTC (Eerdmans, 2008), 224; A. F. Kirkpatrick, *The Book of Psalms* (Cambridge University Press, 1906), 817.

[3] Hence, one of Richard Hays's NT use of the OT criteria is, "Have other readers, both critical and pre-critical, heard the same echoes?" He does clarify that "this criterion should rarely be used as a negative test to exclude proposed echoes that commend themselves on other grounds." Richard B. Hays, *Echoes of Scripture in the Letters of Paul* (Yale University Press, 1989), 30–32.

Availability and Direction

Could the writer of Psalm 145 have alluded to Deut 4:7? Bible readers convinced by traditional conservative authorship arguments have no issue here, because Moses lived and wrote before David lived and wrote.[4] Bible readers convinced by critical reconstructions of the Pentateuch do not always agree on a date for Deuteronomy's final form, but many proposed dates hover around the mid-to-late seventh century BC (leading up to Josiah's reforms).[5] For those who do not think David could have written Psalm 145, Leslie Allen summarizes the field well when he says it is "generally regarded as post-exilic."[6] Therefore, in most dating schema, the writer of Psalm 145 would have been able to access and allude to Deuteronomy 4.

Who borrowed from whom? In this case, Psalm 145 is the most likely borrower for two reasons. First, conservative and critical dating schema put Psalm 145 later, making it the likely borrower. Second, Psalm 145 is a known borrower (we all have those friends) because of Ps 145:8's use of Exod 34:6. Since Ps 145:18 *could have* alluded to Deut 4:7, let's see how it holds up to the three instincts.

---

[4] For a carefully crafted argument that Moses is responsible for all but narrative frames and light updating in Deuteronomy, see Daniel I. Block, "Recovering the Voice of Moses: The Genesis of Deuteronomy," *JETS* 44, no. 3 (September 2001): 385–408.

[5] Though there are detractors, from the early 20th century until the early 21st century many scholars granted that Deuteronomy was compiled at least by 622 BC when King Josiah's reforms described in 2 Kings 22 began. (See, for example, Stephen L. Cook, *Reading Deuteronomy: A Literary and Theological Commentary*, Reading the Old Testament (Smith & Helwys, 2015), 7–9; S. R. Driver, *An Introduction to the Literature of the Old Testament* (Scribner's Sons, 1914), 86.

[6] Leslie C. Allen, *Psalms 101–150*, 2nd ed., WBC 21 (Zondervan, 2018), 297.

Instinct 1: Terms

Psalm 145:18 and Deut 4:7 share two relevant terms, other than the common divine name (*YHWH*). Here are the terms:

Psalm 145:18 ALLUDING TEXT	Deuteronomy 4:7 SOURCE TEXT
The LORD is near [*qārôḇ*] all who call out [*qārā'*] to him, all who call out to him with integrity.	For what great nation is there that has a god near [*qārôḇ*] to it as the LORD our God is to us whenever we call [*qārā'*] to him?

The words are not rare. The Hebrew word for *near* (*qārôḇ*) occurs 76 times in the Old Testament. The Hebrew word for *call* (*qārā'*) occurs 742 times.

Remember that rare terms are not the only way to anchor an allusion. Phrases and word clusters also offer firm anchors. Placing these two Hebrew words alongside one another in an original language search shows that they occur in the same verse only four times in the Old Testament: Deut 4:7; Ps 145:18; Isa 55:6; and Zeph 1:7. Furthermore, the two terms also occur in the same context, though not in the same verse, to refer to prayer and God's nearness in 1 Kgs 8:52, 59; Pss 34:6, 18; 119:145–146, 151; Joel 1:15, 19.[7]

The next instinct will narrow the playing field among this list of texts, but for now, a rare collocation (i.e., word cluster) is sufficient evidence to keep thinking about this proposed allusion.

Instinct 2: Themes

Moving on to *themes*, what resonance does Ps 145:18 have with Deut 4:7? The first place to look is right around the verses themselves, in this case Ps 145:13–21 and Deut 4:1–14. Reading both closely, we find several similarities:

---

[7] Because *qārôḇ* can also refer to physical proximity, I have only listed texts that use the word to refer to God's presence like Ps 145:18 clearly does.

1. Both texts share the theme of listening or hearing (Ps 145:19; Deut 4:1, 13).
2. Both texts share the theme of obedience (Ps 145:18; Deut 4:1–2, 6, 13, 14).
3. Both texts share the theme of God as giver or provider (Ps 145:15–16; Deut 4:1).
4. Both texts share the theme of God destroying the unrepentant (Ps 145:20; Deut 4:3, 26).
5. Both texts share the theme of righteousness (Ps 145:17; Deut 4:7–8).
6. Both texts share the theme of God speaking (Ps 145:13; Deut 4:12–13).

Now, we turn to the themes the broader context of Psalm 145 shares with the broader context of Deut 4:1–40:

1. Both contexts share the theme of greatness (Ps 145:3; Deut 4:6).
2. Both contexts share the theme of teaching (Ps 145:12; Deut 4:9).
3. Both contexts share the theme of descendants (Ps 145:4, 12; Deut 4:9–10).
4. Both contexts share the theme of intergenerational covenantal communication (Ps 145:4; Deut 4:9).
5. Both contexts share the theme of covenantal love (Ps 145:20; Deut 4:37).
6. Both contexts share the theme of God's compassion (Ps 145:8; Deut 4:31).
7. Both contexts share the theme of God as creator (Ps 145:10; Deut 4:32).
8. Both contexts share the theme of the mighty acts of God (Ps 145:5–6, 12; Deut 4:34).
9. Both contexts share the theme of interfacing with non-Israelites (Ps 145:12; Deut 4:7–8, 34).
10. Both contexts share the theme of comprehensiveness, employing the word *all* (*kōl*) with a high frequency.[8]

[8] It appears 17x in Psalm 145 and 23x in Deut 4:1–40.

While studying *terms*, we found two additional texts that contain the same word cluster: Isa 55:5 and Zeph 1:7. Why should Deut 4:7 be more likely a source text than these? To answer that question, we can use a chart to see if those texts share with Psalm 145 the same level of thematic coherence found in Deuteronomy 4.

Alluding Text	**Potential Source Texts**		
Psalm 145	**Deuteronomy 4**	**Isaiah 55**	**Zephaniah 1**
Listening	X	X	-
Obedience	X	-	-
God as Giver	X	X	-
Destruction	X	-	X
Righteousness	X	-	-
God Speaking	X	X	X
Greatness	X	-	X
Teaching	X	-	-
Descendants	X	-	-
Intergenerational	X	-	-
Love	X	X	-
Compassion	X	X	-
Creator	X	-	-
Mighty Acts	X	-	-
Non-Israelites	X	X	X
"All"	X	-	X[9]

Deuteronomy 4 wins. There are also passages where *qārôḇ* and *qārā'* both occur in the same wider context but not in the same verse (1 Kgs 8:52, 59;

[9] It appears 8x in Zephaniah 1 but represents an important theme in Zephaniah: the comprehensiveness of the Day of Yahweh.

Pss 34:6, 18; 119:145–146, 151; Joel 1:15, 19). Do these texts share the same level of thematic correspondence with Psalm 145 as does Deuteronomy 4?

First Kings 8 emerges as a rival to Deuteronomy 4 as the source text. Based on the conservative dating reflected in chapter 2 (fig. 1, p. 37), it would be easy to simply conclude that because Psalm 145 claims to be Davidic it cannot depend on 1 Kings 8. The same point can be demonstrated, however, by considering the allusions in 1 Kings 8 itself. Gary Edward Schnittjer argues persuasively that 1 Kgs 8:15–21 alludes to both Deuteronomy 12 where the Lord says he will choose a place for his name to dwell and 2 Samuel 7 where the Lord chooses David for an eternal dynasty.[10] If 1 Kings 8 draws on both Deuteronomy and material about David, then rather than Psalm 145 drawing from 1 Kings 8, both probably draw from Deuteronomy's theology.

A blend of two of the themes—obedience and righteousness—carries considerable weight in confirming this proposed allusion because they match the sequence in the source text. After the allusion in Ps 145:18a, verse 18b says, "All who call out to him with integrity." "Integrity" here is the Hebrew word *'ĕmeṯ* that connotes faithfulness or truth. Praying with *'ĕmeṯ* means that the people praying are also letting God's grace (v. 8) shape their way of life. The sequence, then, is from prayer to faithful living. The sequence in Ps 145:18 mimics that of Deut 4:7–8,[11] where after talking about God's nearness to praying Israel, verse 8 says, "And what great nation has righteous statutes and ordinances like this entire law I set before you today?" Themes confirm allusions, but themes in a (seemingly) deliberate order offer extra confirmation.

Investigating *themes* supports the claim that Ps 145:18 alludes to Deut 4:7, because of sixteen shared themes. But two questions remain.

---

[10] Gary Edward Schnittjer, *Old Testament Use: A Book-by-Book Guide* (Zondervan, 2021), 195–98.

[11] Jeffery M. Leonard, "Identifying Subtle Allusions: The Promise of Narrative Tracking," *Subtle Citation, Allusion, and Translation in the Hebrew Bible* (Equinox, 2017), 97.

Alluding Text	Potential Source Texts				
Psalm 145	Deuteronomy 4	1 Kings 8	Psalm 34	Psalm 119[12]	Joel 1
Listening	X	X	X	X	X
Obedience	X	X	X	X	-
God as Giver	X	X	X	-	-
Destruction	X	-[13]	X	-	X
Righteousness	X	X	X	-	-
God Speaking	X	X	-	X	X
Greatness	X	X	X	-	-
Teaching	X	-	X	X	-
Descendants	X	X	X	-	-
Intergenerational	X	X	X	-	-
Love	X	X	-	X	-
Compassion	X	X	X	-	-
Creator	X	-	-	-	-
Mighty Acts	X	X	-	-	-
Non-Israelites	X	X	-	-	X
"All"	X	X[14]	-	-	X[15]

[12] The words appear in verses 145–152, a stanza wherein all verses begin with the latter *qoph* ("q").

[13] First Kgs 8:33–40 lists covenant-curse scenarios, but not with the destruction language present in Psalm 145 and Deuteronomy 4.

[14] It appears 36x in 1 Kings 8, emphasizing the collective nature of Solomon's intercession and the temple being dedicated.

[15] It appears 5x in Joel 1, but they are rhetorically significant.

First, why would Psalm 145 allude to Deut 4:7? Second, since allusions are rhetorically significant literary acts, does grasping this allusion help readers make sense of Psalm 145?

Instinct 3: Thesis

We have provided the jury with DNA evidence (*terms*) and explained circumstantial evidence (*themes*), but is there a compelling narrative for why the psalmist committed the allusion? Our four rhetorical-analytical questions facilitate answers to that question.

1. How is the text arranged, and where does the allusion fit?

Psalm 145's title (verse 1 in the Hebrew text [MT]) and the last verse (v. 21) both use the word *tᵊhillâ* (praise). Then verses 1 and 21 also use the word for *bless* (*bārak̲*). When a keyword, or in this case two keywords, occurs near the beginning and end of a biblical text, this is known as *inclusio* or bracketing. It is also a good indicator that the beginning and end have a continuous pericope between them. So, we have a twenty-one-verse pericope framed by the concept of *praise*. This strategic repetition helps readers see the rhetorical goal of the text, so we will have to keep *praise* in mind all throughout.

Additionally, the psalm is laid out in acrostic form, meaning that each verse begins with a letter of the Hebrew alphabet.[16] This literary feature is another strong indicator of the psalm's rhetorical goals for at least two reasons. First, acrostics serve a teaching function.[17] Old Testament

---

[16] Except for the notoriously absent verse for the letter *nun* (*n*), verse 13b in the CSB. As noted previously, the free NET textual notes present the issues concisely and evenhandedly. Most modern English translations contain a footnote briefly stating the issue.

[17] While all Scripture is "profitable for teaching" (2 Tim 3:16), Hebrew acrostics may have served as memory aids in teaching contexts. M. J. van Eijzeren

acrostics aren't there to be cute (though, if we're honest, they're adorable), but to communicate something by their very presence.[18] What is this psalm trying to teach? (Question 3 addresses this more fully but based on the psalm's brackets we know it has something to do with *praise*.) Second, acrostics convey what we would call in English an A-to-Z flavor.[19] Comprehensiveness would make sense in a psalm that uses the Hebrew word for *all* (*kōl*) seventeen times in twenty-one verses! Adele Berlin, Avigdor Shinan, and Benjamin Sommer state the rhetorical effect well, "This A-to-Z function is even more relevant in our psalm [145], for it is about infinite praise to God. Though the speaker cannot list all possible words of praise, the structure of the alphabet—from which all words are formed—summons all potential words" to create a "catalog of praise."[20]

Sometimes there is more to an acrostic poem's layout than the alphabet alone, so it helps to trace how the psalm's poetic argument for total praise unfolds. Berlin writes—and this can be said of other biblical genres too—that to "understand how a poem is constructed is to begin to understand what it expresses."[21] We already know that the *inclusio* of

---

catalogues thirteen existing scholarly proposals for the origin and purpose of Hebrew acrostic poetry, and you may notice the educational flavor of several of them: (1) "completeness," (2) "mnemonic," (3) "stylistic," (4) "display of skill," (5) orderliness, (6) "enhancement of the message," (7) "magic," (8) teaching aid, (9) "embedded message," (10) interpretive aid, (11) "responsive structuring," (12) dedicatory, and (13) "authorship." M. J. van Eijzeren, "'Halbnachts steh' ich auf': An Exploration into the Translation of Biblical Acrostics" (MA Thesis, Utrecht University, 2012), 30–37.

[18] C. J. Fantuzzo states memorably that Hebrew acrostics are "communicative," not "merely ornamental." C. J. Fantuzzo, "Acrostic," *Dictionary of the Old Testament: Wisdom, Poetry & Writings* (IVP Academic, 2010), 3.

[19] Fantuzzo, 4.

[20] Adele Berlin, Avigdor Shinan, and Benjamin D. Sommer, *Psalms 120–150*, JPS Bible Commentary (Jewish Publication Society, 2023), 141–42.

[21] Adele Berlin, "The Rhetoric of Psalm 145," in *Biblical and Related Studies Presented to Samuel Iwry*, ed. Ann Kort and Scott Morschauser (Eisenbrauns, 1985), 18.

the word *bless* is a part of the structure, but Rueven Kimelman helpfully notes that the word occurs in the center of the psalm also as something like an interlude (v. 10).[22] When the beginning, middle, and end of a poem contain the same keyword, this sometimes indicates the presence of a **chiasm**,[23] or an X-shaped structure wherein inner and outer sections match in pairs with an unmatched point being isolated in the center. The resulting structure looks something like this:

A Introductory **blessing** (*bārak̲*, 2x) by the psalmist (title–v. 2)[24]
    B Description of the Lord's greatness (v. 3)
        C Intergenerational proclamation of the Lord's works (vv. 4–7)
            D Description of the Lord's attributes (vv. 8–9)
                X Central **blessing** (*bārak̲*) by all creation (v. 10)
            D' Description of the Lord's kingdom (vv. 11–13a)
        C' International enjoyment of the Lord's provision (vv. 13b–16)
    B' Description of the Lord's relationality (vv. 17–20)
A' Concluding **blessing** (*bārak̲*) by all flesh (v. 21)[25]

---

[22] Rueven Kimelman, "Psalm 145: Theme, Structure, and Impact," *JBL* 113, no. 1 (1994): 38.

[23] Craig Blomberg argues that the plausibility of a proposed chiasm increases when a central theme is repeated in the first and last sections of a passage or larger block of text. Craig Blomberg, "The Structure of 2 Corinthians 1–7," *CTR* 4, no. 1 (1989): 7.

[24] I agree with James Hamilton that because the title and v. 21 both contain *tᵊhillâ* (praise), the title is integral to the structure of the psalm and therefore probably original. James M. Hamilton Jr., *Psalms*, vol. 2, Evangelical Biblical Theology Commentary (Lexham, 2021), 492–93.

[25] Once the first, middle, and last verses are noted, we are left with two remaining sections: verses 3–9 and 11–20. Pronoun shifts assist in further delineating verses 3–9 into three sections: (1) verse 3 refers to the Lord in the third person, (2) verses 4–7 in the second person, and (3) verses 8–9 return to the third person. Pronouns delineate verses 11–20 also: the Lord is addressed in the second person in verses 11–13a, verses 13b–14 shift to third person but thematically fit with verses 15–16, which return to second person pronouns, and then verses 17–20 employ third person pronouns.

The proposed allusion occurs in a section about God's relational nature: he is near to his praying people (v. 18), he satisfies the desires of his praying people (v. 19), he guards and vindicates his people (v. 20).

Why does it matter that the allusion occurs in verses 17–20? It matters for at least three reasons. First, the section pairs with verse 3 in the chiasm, and verse 3 asserts the *greatness* of Yahweh. Kimelman argues that the psalm alternates between lauding God's transcendence (or, greatness) and immanence (or, nearness).[26] Verse 18 contributes to the portrayal of a God who is *near* even though he is *great*. Second, the pairing intensifies one of the themes noted under the second instinct. Deuteronomy 4:7 asks what other nation is so *great* (*gāḏôl*) as the one with a God just a prayer away. The same Hebrew word, *gāḏôl*, occurs in Ps 145:3 with another word from the same root meaning "greatness" (*gᵊḏûlâ*). So enthralled with Yahweh is the psalmist that he transposes the greatness in Deut 4:7 onto God—and does so in a verse that pairs structurally (i.e., the chiasm) and thematically (i.e., the transcendence/immanence juxtaposition) with the allusion to Deut 4:7.[27]

Third, verse 18's allusion creates symmetry with the way the rest of the psalm uses other Scripture. Everyone recognizes verse 8's allusion to Exod 34:6:

---

[26] Kimelman, "Psalm 145," 46. See Stanley J. Grenz, David Guretzki, and Cherith Fee Nordling, *Pocket Dictionary of Theological Terms*, IVP Pocket Reference Series (InterVarsity, 1999), "immanence."

[27] Deuteronomy 4 also vividly ascribes greatness to Yahweh's deeds in verses 32–38.

Psalm 145:8 ALLUDING TEXT	Exodus 34:6 SOURCE TEXT
The LORD [*Yahweh*] is gracious [*ḥannûn*] and compassionate [*raḥûm*], slow [*'ārēḵ*] to anger [*'ap̄*] and great [*gāḏôl*] in faithful love [*ḥeseḏ*].	The LORD [*Yahweh*] passed in front of him and proclaimed: The LORD [*Yahweh*]—the LORD [*Yahweh*] is a compassionate [*ḥannûn*] and gracious [*raḥûm*] God, slow [*'ārēḵ*] to anger [*'ap̄*] and abounding in faithful love [*ḥeseḏ*] and truth.

Additionally, Frank-Lothar Hossfeld and Erich Zenger argue that there are two allusions to material from earlier in the flow of the Psalter.[28] The first is a phrase in Ps 145:3 that comes from either Ps 48:1 or Ps 96:4:

Psalm 145:3 ALLUDING TEXT	Psalm 48:1a and 96:4 SOURCE TEXT
The LORD [*Yahweh*] is great [*gāḏôl*] and is highly [*mᵊ'ōḏ*] praised [*hālal*]; his greatness is unsearchable.	The LORD [*Yahweh*] is great [*gāḏôl*] and highly [*mᵊ'ōḏ*] praised [*hālal*] in the city of our God (46:1a). For the LORD [*Yahweh*] is great [*gāḏôl*] and is highly [*mᵊ'ōḏ*] praised [*hālal*]; he is feared above all gods (96:4).

[28] Frank-Lothar Hossfeld and Erich Zenger, *Psalms 3*, Hermeneia (Fortress, 2011), 597.

The second occurs in Ps 145:15–16:

Psalm 145:15–16 ALLUDING TEXT[29]	Psalm 104:27–28 SOURCE TEXT
All [*kōl*] eyes look [*śāḇar*] to you, and you give [*nāṯan*] them their food [*ʾōḵel*] at the proper time [*ʿēṯ*]. You open [*pāṯaḥ*] your hand [*yāḏ*] and satisfy [*śāḇaʿ*] the desire of every living thing.	All [*kōl*] of them wait [*śāḇar*] for you to give [*nāṯan*] them their food [*ʾōḵel*] at the right time [*ʿēṯ*]. When you give it to them, they gather it; when you open [*pāṯaḥ*] your hand [*yāḏ*], they are satisfied [*śāḇaʿ*] with good things.

If the proposal here is correct, that Ps 145:18 alludes to Deut 4:7, then it is the final installment in a symmetrical set of allusions in the psalm: The psalmist alludes to a psalm text and a written Torah text before the psalm's chiastic center and then to a psalm and written Torah text after the center. The two allusions in the first half of the psalm relate to the Lord's character, and the two allusions in the second half of the psalm relate to his condescension to interact with his creation. They fit in the psalm's structure like this:

A Introductory blessing (*bāraḵ*, 2x) by the psalmist (title–v. 2)
  B Description of the Lord's greatness (v. 3) **psalm allusion**
    C Intergenerational proclamation of the Lord's works (vv. 4–7)
      D Description of the Lord's attributes (vv. 8–9) **Torah allusion**
        X Central blessing (*bāraḵ*) by all creation (v. 10)
      D' Description of the Lord's kingdom (vv. 11–13a)
    C' International enjoyment of the Lord's provision (vv. 13b–16) **psalm allusion**
  B' Description of the Lord's relationality (vv. 17–20) **Torah allusion**
A' Concluding blessing (*bāraḵ*) by all flesh (v. 21)

[29] Schnittjer considers this overlap in wording to result from the use of a liturgical stock phrase. Schnittjer, *Old Testament Use*, 545. Whether he is right or Hossfeld and Zenger are, this phrase references psalms material that readers of the Psalter would have encountered both in Pss 48:1 and 96:4.

The rhetoric of Psalm 145 unfolds in an orderly manner fitting to an acrostic poem. The stately poem marches through reasons to praise the Lord and then, in its penultimate section, alludes to Deut 4:7. Question 4 will explore the reason, but for now, alluding to Deut 4:7 embeds in the psalm an additional reason to praise: God is doing in response to the psalm's praise activity what he said he would do in Deut 4:7.

2. What general human condition or spiritual condition does the text address?

In the 1950s, J. B. Phillips wrote *Your God Is Too Small* and concluded that "we can never have too big a conception of God."[30] Psalm 145 aims at humanity's tendency to reduce God and slacken our worship of him. Psalm 145 exists because we do not automatically perceive the grandeur of the Lord's character and respond to him worshipfully. Why would believers need to be recalibrated to praising the Lord's grandeur? Psalmists used praise as what rhetoric professor Davida Charney calls "regular maintenance work" for Israel because "even at the best of times, Israelite speakers are well aware of the precariousness of their paths and the need to use praise activity to maintain their balance."[31] God's people needed Psalm 145 to be written to motivate praise with the all-encompassing grandeur of God's character and activity in the world.

3. What is the alluding text's persuasive goal for the situation it addresses?

Psalm 145 exists because—without the intervention of biblical texts like this one—worship doesn't.[32] I agree with Adele Berlin that Psalm 145 "is

---

[30] J. B. Phillips, *Your God is Too Small*, repr. ed. (Wyvern, 1957), 123.

[31] Davida Charney, *Persuading God: Rhetorical Studies of First-Person Psalms*, Hebrew Bible Monographs 73 (Sheffield Phoenix, 2017), 18–20.

[32] I intentionally allude here to John Piper's famous line, "Missions exists because *worship* doesn't." John Piper, *Let the Nations Be Glad: The Supremacy of God in Missions*, 3rd ed. (Baker Academic, 2010), 230.

a poetic 'argument' aimed at persuading the hearer to do what the psalmist has done, namely, praise the Lord always."[33] It helps to consult scholarly works on the alluding text to see if they generally agree with the way one is reading the text's rhetorical goal(s). But how does it persuade readers to praise the Lord always? Returning, then, to the threefold rhetorical aim of all biblical texts (repent, believe, or obey), Psalm 145 urges obedience to a call to praise (i.e., deliberative rhetoric).[34] Graciously, rather than merely telling God's people to praise God, Psalm 145 parades the attributes, transcendence, kingdom, and massiveness of God before the reader to allow them to be swept up and, as German author Erhard Gerstenberger articulates, "feel part of God's sovereign rule of justice and equity."[35]

4. How does the source text assist the alluding text in its persuasive goal?

The psalm marches through reasons to praise God with encyclopedic precision. Here are the main reasons the psalm provides for praising God:

---

[33] Berlin, "Rhetoric," 21.

[34] Ryan Cook demonstrates that, in the broadest rhetorical categories, praise psalms align with epideictic rhetoric because they seek to instill particular values in the hearer. Ryan J. Cook, *The Rhetoric of Praise: Prayer and Persuasion in the Psalms*, GlossaHouse Dissertation Series 6 (GlossaHouse, 2018), 222–24. In this sense, Psalm 145 seeks to persuade hearers to believe certain things about God. Alongside this persuasive goal, however, v. 21 seeks to involve its hearers in the psalmist's praise activity: "Let every living thing bless his holy name." Whereas some translations take this to be a future tense verb (called an "imperfect verb"), describing what will happen (e.g., NASB: "all flesh will bless"), most translations render the verb as a prescriptive statement (called a "jussive verb") of what ought to happen (i.e., "let"). This invitational conclusion to the psalm suggests that the epideictic belief content of the psalm is aimed at a deliberative action on the part of faithful hearers: join in with the psalmist's praise. As will be discussed later, this seems to be how the compilers of the Psalter understood Psalm 145 since it initiates the book's grand finale of praise (Psalms 146–150).

[35] Erhard Gerstenberger, *Psalms, Part 2 and Lamentations*, FOTL 15 (Eerdmans, 2001), 436.

- He is "the King" (v. 1).
- He is "great" in an "unsearchable" way (v. 3).
- He has a multigenerational track record of "awe-inspiring acts" (vv. 4–6).
- He is good and righteous (v. 7).
- He is, as revealed to Moses on Mount Sinai, still "gracious and compassionate, slow to anger and great in faithful love" (v. 8, alluding to Exod 34:6).
- He is impartially "good" to his creation (vv. 9–10).
- His kingdom is glorious and unending (vv. 11–13).
- He "helps" the "oppressed" (v. 14).
- He provides sustenance for his creation (vv. 15–16).
- He is "faithful in all his acts" (v. 17).
- He is "near" to his praying people (v. 18).
- He satisfies and saves those who take refuge in him (v. 19).
- He protects his people and judges his enemies (v. 20).

What does an allusion to Deut 4:7 add to this already impressive list? At least three things.

First, it adds a reason to praise God: because he commissioned Israel's cries to be a vehicle of his nearness. Second, the prayers and cries that originated to distinguish God's people from other nations is now something that *all* (17x in Psalm 145) creation—including those other nations—are invited into. The psalmist has already done this with the well-recognized allusion in verse 8 to Exod 34:6—that classic expression of Yahweh's attributes that comforted Moses in the wake of Israel's golden calf failure. The psalmist, not unlike Jonah 4:2's use of Exod 34:6–7 but with a better attitude, takes Israel's confession and applies it "to everyone" (v. 9a).[36] Likewise, the nations who would be mystified by Yahweh's nearness to Israel in Deut 4:7 can now benefit by crying out to him in truth (like the present Gentile author). This explains the

[36] Craig C. Broyles, *Psalms*, UBCS (Baker, 2012), 507.

psalmist's transformation of Deut 4:7's "great nation" (i.e., Israel) calling on him now being "all who call out to him" (Ps 145:18a). Third, integrating the first and second reasons, praising God fulfills a Mosaic commission *and* an evangelistic mission. Calling out to God would catch the eye of other nations in Deut 4:7, and it has become the vehicle to invite them into Yahweh's nearness in Psalm 145. Alluding to Deut 4:7, it turns out, adds quite a kick to the rhetoric of Psalm 145. Tim Mackie brilliantly calls Old Testament allusions "hyperlinks" to other biblical texts.[37] Like a news article that links other articles because it cannot fit all the necessary information, Psalm 145 catalogues reasons to praise the Lord and then embeds so-called hyperlinks for readers to click, read, and find additional reasons to praise.

If I am right about this allusion, it might help us understand the book of Psalms as well. In the 1980s, Gerald Wilson started a fruitful trend of looking at the arrangement of the biblical psalms with an eye toward their bookwide structure and flow. He noticed something that many interpreters have echoed since: Psalm 145 occupies a unique position in the Psalter. He writes, "Ps 145 stands as the 'climax' of the fifth book of the Psalter, with the final *hallel* (Pss 146–150) drawing its impetus from 145:21."[38] Psalms 146–150 are sometimes called the Final Hallel because they contain a high concentration of the command *hallelujah* (lit., *y'all praise Yah*) and possess a sweeping, cosmic scope. They are like the grand finale of the Psalter fireworks show. Psalm 145, then, does two things: (1) it concludes the normal operations of the Book of Psalms before the finale and, as Wilson says, (2) in verse 21 lights the match that sets off the finale.

---

[37] Tim Mackie, Classroom Sneak Peek: Jonah, *BibleProject Podcast*, episode 3, "Hyperlinks and Patterns in Jonah," The Bible Project, September 6, 2021, https://bibleproject.com/podcast/hyperlinks-and-patterns-jonah/.

[38] Gerald H. Wilson, *The Editing of the Hebrew Psalter*, SBL Dissertation Series 76 (Scholars, 1985), 225.

Psalm 145's title—"A psalm of praise. Of David."—also sets it apart, for two reasons. First, it is the last psalm with David's name in the superscription. Therefore, the psalm brings to a close the seventy-three-psalm witness of the chief psalmist. Second, it is the only psalm with the word *praise* (*tᵊhillâ*) in its title. The plural form of this word became the Hebrew title for the whole book: *Tehillim*. Psalm 145 is so pivotal for the Psalter, that J. Clinton McCann writes, "It is even possible that the Psalter originally ended with Psalm 145" before the grand finale was added by the Spirit-inspired person(s) that compiled the book into its final form.[39]

Why read off Psalm 145's résumé like this? The late Patrick Miller suggested that the book of Psalms presents the prayers prescribed in Deut 4:7.[40] What if Psalm 145 alludes to Deut 4:7 to punctuate the book by showing that it exists because of Deut 4:7's claim that God is near when his people call? The book testifies to the beauty and grace of Deut 4:7 and then ends with a nod to the verse as its prayer commission. Eugene Peterson once wrote that the five books of the Psalms are an "antiphonal" response to the five books of Torah. That is, God speaks in the Torah and his people respond in the Psalter.[41] The allusion to Deut 4:7 may confirm Peterson's claim. God spoke through Moses that he will be near when his people call, and Ps 145:18 celebrates the ongoing fulfillment of Moses's words.

Some readers might not be convinced that Psalm 145 alludes to Deut 4:7. Herein lies the beauty of studying the Bible's use of the Bible: at best, you uncover an intentional and interpretively significant allusion; at worst, you place two biblical texts in conversation with one another and see both in a new light.

---

[39] J. Clinton McCann, "Psalms," *New Interpreter's Bible* 3 (Abingdon, 2015), 711.

[40] Patrick D. Miller, "Deuteronomy and Psalms: Evoking a Biblical Conversation," *JBL* 118, no. 1 (1999): 8.

[41] Eugene H. Peterson, *Answering God: The Psalms as Tools for Prayer* (HarperSanFrancisco, 1989), 53.

Practicing the Abbreviated Instincts

Alluding Text: Psalm 145:18 **Source Text:** Deuteronomy 4:7		
Instinct 1: Terms	☐ Rare Terms ☐ Uncommon Phrases ☒ Unique Clusters	*Explain:* The Hebrew word for *near* (*qārôḇ*) occurs 76x in the Old Testament. The Hebrew word for *call* (*qārāʾ*) occurs 742x. As a unique cluster, they only occur together in the same verse 4x (Deut 4:7; Ps 145:18; Isa 55:6; Zeph 1:7).
Instinct 2: Themes	*Both Immediate Contexts:* 1. Listening or hearing (Ps 145:19; Deut 4:1, 13) 2. Obedience (Ps 145:18; Deut 4:1–2, 6, 13, 14) 3. God as giver or provider (Ps 145:15–16; Deut 4:1) 4. God destroying the unrepentant (Ps 145:20; Deut 4:3, 26) 5. Righteousness (Ps 145:17; Deut 4:7–8) 6. God speaking (Ps 145:13; Deut 4:12–13)	*Both Broad Contexts:* 1. Greatness (Ps 145:3; Deut 4:6) 2. Teaching (Ps 145:12; Deut 4:9) 3. Descendants (Ps 145:4, 12; Deut 4:9–10) 4. Intergenerational covenantal communication (Ps 145:4; Deut 4:9) 5. Covenantal love (Ps 145:20; Deut 4:37) 6. God's compassion (Ps 145:8; Deut 4:31) 7. God as creator (Ps 145:10; Deut 4:32) 8. Mighty acts of God (Ps 145:5–6, 12; Deut 4:34) 9. Non-Israelites (Ps 145:12; Deut 4:7–8, 34) 10. Comprehensiveness ("all" 17x in Psalm 145; 23x in Deuteronomy 4)

Instinct 3: Thesis	1) *How is the text arranged, and where does the allusion occur?*
	A Introductory blessing by the psalmist (title–v. 2)
	  B Description of the Lord's greatness (v. 3)
	    C Intergenerational proclamation of the Lord's works (vv. 4–7)
	      D Description of the Lord's attributes (vv. 8–9)
	        X Central blessing by all creation (v. 10)
	      D' Description of the Lord's kingdom (vv. 11–13a)
	    C' International enjoyment of the Lord's provision (vv. 13b–16)
	  B' Description of the Lord's relationality (vv. 17–20)
	A' Concluding blessing by all flesh (v. 21)
	The allusion occurs in the section about Yahweh's relational nature (vv. 17–20) that is chiastically paired with verse 3, which emphasizes his greatness. This (1) juxtaposes transcendence (v. 3) and nearness (vv. 17–20), and (2) matches the greatness-nearness theme in the source text.

	2) *What general human situation or spiritual condition does the text address?* Psalm 145 addresses the human tendency to slacken worship by restrictive views of God or his activity in the world by offering a grand vision of his character and kingdom.
	3) *What is the text's persuasive goal for the situation it addresses?* ☐ Repent ☐ Believe ☒ Obey *Explain:* A call to praise that parades the attributes, transcendence, kingdom, and massiveness of God before the reader to allow them to be swept up in the nearness (v. 18) that comes through calling upon him in praise.
	4) *How does the source text assist the alluding text in its persuasive goal?* (1) Another reason to praise (commissioning Israel's cries as a vehicle of God's nearness); (2) prayerful cries that were unique to Israel (Deut 4:7) are now available to "all" (Ps 145:18a); (3) reconceiving Deut 4:7's commission as invitational/evangelistic; and (4) framing the Psalter as responsive to Deut 4:7.

Conclusion

I hope this chapter's sample leaves you with two impressions about identifying and analyzing Old Testament allusions. First, the instincts fit into normal exegetical procedures. Elements of the process like identifying contextual themes and outlining a passage are probably familiar to you. In some ways, the instincts utilize interpretive skills you already possess but then marshal them in a deliberate direction (i.e., analyzing connections between two texts). Second, the instincts enhance standard exegetical procedures. When an allusion is grasped, it provides a new vista for surveying the message of a biblical text. Embedded allusions, and the work it takes to grasp them, remind me of Prov 25:2: "It is the glory of God to conceal a matter / and the glory of kings to investigate a matter." I like what the Reformer Philipp Melancthon says about this verse: "This proverb reminds us that the word of God is a hidden wisdom, only to be acquired with great effort."[42]

---

[42] Philipp Melanchthon, "Seeking Hidden Wisdom," in *Proverbs, Ecclesiastes, Song of Songs*, RCOS 9 (InterVarsity, 2023), 160.

7

Instincts in Action: Teaching and Preaching Old Testament Allusions

Introduction

Nobody wants "impoverished preaching." Recently, I heard a biblical scholar diagnose something that he believes is leading to *impoverished preaching*. If you're reading this book, I doubt you want to preach impoverished sermons or, for teachers like me, you don't want impoverished lectures or assessments. Here was his diagnosis: "I am astounded how many times I hear a sermon on a New Testament text that includes a quotation [from the OT]—[we] won't even talk about allusions . . . it amazes me how many times a preacher will preach a passage that contains a quotation and they don't do anything with it."[1] If preachers ignore

[1] Benjamin Gladd made this remark in a podcast interview: "G. K. Beale and Benjamin Gladd–Dictionary of the New Testament Use of the Old Testament," Guilt, Grace, Gratitude Podcast, November 23, 2023, https://www.youtube.com/watch?v=P7eostbSNJ4.

the NT's use of the OT, then we can safely assume that the problem is worse for the OT use of the OT.[2] This chapter is meant to encourage anyone with a teaching or preaching ministry to consider integrating the Old Testament's use of the Old Testament as a steady feature of their presentation of Old Testament texts.

Advantages to Both Teaching and Preaching the Old Testament Use of the Old Testament[3]

Before talking about advantages to the teaching and preaching crafts respectively, here are four reasons that all Bible teaching can be strengthened by giving attention to allusions in the Old Testament. First, Old Testament allusions exemplify how biblical authors communicated the Bible to their audience. Noticing how biblical writers contextualized and communicated Scripture can provide meaningful models for contextualizing and communicating Scripture today. For example, how should a teacher or preacher encourage Christians to apply Exod 34:6–7 to their

---

[2] On the already diminished attention the Old Testament receives in contemporary preaching, see Brent A. Strawn, *The Old Testament is Dying: A Diagnosis and Recommended Treatment*, Theological Explorations for the Catholic Church (Baker Academic, 2017), 4–5.

[3] The four reasons listed are germane to teaching and preaching in general, but I want to mention an added theological benefit: grasping the oft debated New Testament use of the Old Testament. I cannot improve upon or add anything to the robust recent discussion by Matthew Harmon and Gary Schnittjer on the topic, so I highly recommend reading chapter 1 in their *How to Study the Bible's Use of the Bible*. Increased attention to the OT use of the OT can and should be a game changer for the study of the NT use of the OT. Harmon and Schnittjer argue persuasively that the NT writers' approach to the OT is far more formed by the hermeneutical instincts they perceive in the OT writers' use of Scripture than by Second Temple Judaism. Matthew S. Harmon and Gary Edward Schnittjer, *How to Study the Bible's Use of the Bible: Seven Hermeneutical Choices for the Old and New Testaments* (Zondervan Academic, 2024).

lives? The way biblical writers allude to and utilize Exod 34:6–7 provides several inspired options for application:

- interceding for unrepentant people like Num 14:18
- resolving to testify to Yahweh's gracious deeds like Isa 63:7
- calling to repentance like Hos 1:4–6; 2:19–20; Joel 2:13; Ps 32:5; 2 Chr 30:9
- facilitating corporate intercession and repentance like Neh 9:17, 31
- confronting nationalistic prejudice like the narrator's perspective in Jonah 4:2[4]
- praising Yahweh like Mic 7:18; Pss 103:8; 111:4; 145:8
- hoping for God's judgment of oppressive governments like Nah 1:2–3
- lamenting the apparent absence of God's intervention in suffering like Ps 86:15
- lamenting and finding hope in collective suffering like Lam 3:22–23.[5]

This application list is far thicker than any I could have concocted on my own if I were teaching or preaching on Exod 34:6–7. I can trace my passion for inner-biblical allusions back to a 2012 lecture series by Paul House on this passage and its use throughout the rest of the Old Testament, in which House noted that the use and reuse of texts like

[4] Jonah alludes to Exod 34:6–7 as he laments Nineveh receiving God's mercy; the book of Jonah uses this scene to confront the hatred of enemies.

[5] These allusions are derived from the work of Derek D. Bass, "Hosea's Use of Scripture: An Analysis of His Hermeneutics," (PhD diss., Southern Baptist Theological Seminary, 2008), 257; James M. Hamilton Jr., *God's Glory in Salvation Through Judgment: A Biblical Theology* (Crossway, 2010), 134–36; Gary Edward Schnittjer, *Old Testament Use of the Old Testament: A Book-by-Book Guide* (Zondervan, 2021), 877.

Exod 34:6–7 show Bible readers "how subsequent writers preached and taught and wrote about Scripture."[6]

Second, Old Testament allusions battle biblical illiteracy by demonstrating canonical connectivity. One of today's foremost evangelical advocates for pursuing biblical literacy in the American church is Jen Wilkin. She defines biblical literacy as occurring "when a person has access to a Bible in a language she understands and is steadily moving toward knowledge and understanding of the text."[7] Among the poor Bible reading habits that keep biblical literacy low, she lists what she calls "the Jack Sprat Approach": picky reading that inevitably avoids the Old Testament except for Psalms (though I think most of those are avoided too), Proverbs, and a few popular narratives.[8] Wilkin wisely diagnoses avoidance of the Old Testament as a malnourishing factor in biblical literacy. How could biblical literacy be anything but anemic while avoiding the 75 percent of God's Word found in the Old Testament?[9] And how can the New Testament be understood in the present state of affairs, given its constant quotations and allusions to the Old Testament?

What can be done to get American Christians' noses and hearts back into the pages of the Old Testament? The modern evangelical biblical theology movement has helped tremendously, with the likes of Graeme Goldsworthy and D. A. Carson training pastors to show congregants

---

[6] Paul R. House, "God's Character in God's Word (Exodus 34:1–10, 27)," 2012 Biblical Studies Lectures, Beeson Divinity School, February 14, 2012, https://www.youtube.com/watch?v=fhxLc3owd9E, 4:27–4:52.

[7] Jen Wilkin, *Women of the Word: How to Study the Bible with Both Our Hearts and Our Minds*, 2nd ed. (Crossway, 2019), 24.

[8] Wilkin, *Women of the Word*, 25–27. For a summary of sociological research that supports Wilkin's anecdotal assessment, see Strawn, *Old Testament Is Dying*, 20–27. For example, 41 percent of professing Christians know who Job is in the Bible, compared to 42 percent of atheists/agnostics.

[9] This percentage is based on the total word count of the Bible, calculated by Jason S. DeRouchie, *Delighting in the Old Testament: Through Christ and For Christ* (Crossway, 2024), 3.

the cross-testament connectivity that exists in the Bible. I would like to suggest another strategy: show students and congregants how the Old Testament uses the Old Testament. My pastor, Scott Markley, did this for First Baptist Church of Lake Wales while preaching on Psalm 68. Concerning verse 1, Markley explained that David refers there to Num 10:35.[10] Most Christians avoid the book of Numbers, but this brief explanation provided the congregation with a cognitive connection point between David's life and Israel's departure from Sinai. Explanations like this, over time, build biblical literacy pathways to various points in the Old Testament.

Third, Old Testament allusions sometimes clarify tough texts. Protestants have long recognized, in something called the *analogia fidei* (analogy of faith), that Scripture is its own best interpreter. What I mean here, however, is a bit more specific because allusions are Spirit-inspired, author-intended connections to another passage. Where the analogy of faith seeks a clear passage, studying allusions seeks the intended partner passage. Speaking of tough texts, few Old Testament texts surpass the imprecatory psalms (i.e., psalms that ask God to judge enemies of God). The grisliest of them all is Psalm 137, prayed against Babylon, where the climax of the psalm is its final verse: "Happy is he who takes your little ones / and dashes them against the rocks" (v. 9). The word *dash* (*nāp̄aṣ*) occurs in thirteen Old Testament texts but only one other time in the Psalms. In Ps 2:9, Yahweh's royal Son will defeat his enemies and "will shatter [*nāp̄aṣ*] them like pottery." Trevor Laurence argues that the psalmist, then, prays in Psalm 137 "for an Israelite king who will function climactically (even eschatologically) as the son of God, actually administering the shattering judgment" promised at the Psalter's outset.[11] All

[10] Scott Markley, "A Song for the Victorious: Psalm 68," First Baptist Church of Lake Wales, August 27, 2023, https://www.youtube.com/watch?v=EelM0nGy0Zo.

[11] Trevor Laurence, "Serpent Seen and Son of God: The Enemy and the Imprecator in the Psalms of Vengeance," *CTR* 17, no. 2 (Spring 2020): 119. I am

tension does not dissipate from Psalm 137, but if the psalm asks the coming Davidic Messiah to mete out judgment, then it is no more tense than the Root of David conquering enemies in Rev 5:5.

Fourth, Old Testament allusions sometimes allow readers to reengage overfamiliar texts. For example, from childhood many churchgoers learn the narratives in Daniel. I recall multiple cartoon renditions (both human and vegetative). Joshua Philpot argues persuasively, employing *terms* and *themes*, that Daniel narratives—especially Daniel 2's dream interpretation passage—allude to the Joseph dream interpretation narratives.[12] The result is a new vista on a well-known story's *thesis*: Daniel is a "new Joseph . . . on the cusp of a new exodus."[13] This not only adds depth to presenting the Daniel narratives, but it increases people's awareness of canonical connections within the Old Testament. With these four advantages to teaching and preaching Old Testament allusions, I would like to explore advantages that are specific to the teaching and preaching crafts.

Advantages to Teaching the Old Testament Use of the Old Testament

I taught for years before receiving formal training in educational theory. Nevertheless, in the Lord's kindness I always had either a boss or a senior colleague from whom I imbibed pedagogical wisdom.[14] My

---

less convinced than Laurence that the "little ones" (*ʿôlēl*) refer to the offspring (*zeraʿ*) of the serpent referred to in Gen 3:15 because the connection lacks the terms to be a convincing proposed allusion.

[12] Joshua M. Philpot, "Was Joseph a Type of Daniel? Typological Correspondence in Genesis 37–50 and Daniel 1–6," *JETS* 61, no. 4 (2018): 688.

[13] Philpot, 696.

[14] I'm thinking here of two men. My first boss was Jeff Wilcox, a brilliant educator who taught me what I needed to know to run a classroom and keep a gradebook. The second was a colleague-turned-supervisor named Caswell McWaters. To this day, I employ wisdom in the classroom gained from these two godly men.

first boss taught me how to write lesson plans by orienting me to a tool called Bloom's Taxonomy. This tool categorizes learning objectives, activities, and assessments by whether they cultivate lower order skills (e.g., recall or definition), higher order skills (e.g., analysis or synthesis), or the highest order skills (e.g., defense or evaluation).[15] Various revisions have been proposed, various tables and visualizations exist online, and alternative tools are available, but the basic notion seems persistent: some learning activities do not require advanced thinking, and educators want to help students develop into more advanced thinking. The earliest iteration of the taxonomy placed the following three skills at the three highest tiers: analysis, synthesis, and evaluation.[16] Notice that the three instincts in this book provide a trajectory moving upward along those tiers:

Bloom's Taxonomy	**Inner-Biblical Instincts**
Analysis	Terms (analyze relevant shared language and whether rarity or clustering indicate evidence for an allusion)
Synthesis	Themes (correlate the texts and their contexts to gather confirmatory overlap between the texts)
Evaluation	Thesis (generate an account of the passage's overall rhetoric and the contribution of the allusion to that rhetoric)

Because the three instincts provide repetition and movement along the taxonomy of learning, they provide ideal activities for in-class assignments,

[15] Susan Wallace, ed., *A Dictionary of Education*, 2nd ed. (Oxford University Press, 2015), 37–38.

[16] See Faculty Center, "Bloom's Taxonomy, University of Central Florida website, accessed February 24, 2025, https://fctl.ucf.edu/teaching-resources/course-design/blooms-taxonomy/.

group work, research/exegetical papers, and student presentations. In a class on Judges, for example, students worked through the instincts in a worksheet and then presented their findings to the class informally. In a class on Scripture's use of Scripture, students wrote extended papers employing the instincts and then presented the results to the class in formal presentations. Although I do not use these assignments in Old Testament Survey courses, I find that in lectures, pointing out allusions throughout the Old Testament provides the advantages listed in the previous section.

Notes on Communicating Old Testament Allusions

In closing, I would like to suggest a process for preaching and teaching from Old Testament allusions. First, as you acquaint yourself with the text, note anything in the text that reminds you of another Old Testament text. Cross-references in a good study Bible can help here too. Perhaps you'll see an otherwise unnoticed allusion. Second, check strategic sources. Unfortunately, many commentaries overlook Old Testament allusions.[17] I recommend reading the relevant Bible book entry in the *Dictionary of the New Testament Use of the Old Testament* and the relevant section in Schnittjer's *Old Testament Use of Old Testament*.[18] Perhaps there will be a recognized allusion to guide your exposition. Third, if your intuition or the strategic sources suggest an allusion, work through the three instincts in this book to grasp if and how the alluding text uses the source text. If it turns out that there is not an allusion, then the time has not been lost because you have been thinking about the relationship of two biblical texts that can also strengthen exposition in the spirit of the analogy of

[17] Owing to the youth of the field and to the often cursory nature of many commentaries that simply cannot chase down every inner-biblical connection.

[18] Be sure not only to check the body of each chapter in this source but also the "filters" at the end of each chapter for potential allusions that did not meet Schnittjer's criteria of representing exegetical advances on their source texts. For a bit more on this, see my discussion of his method in the preface.

faith. Fourth, use your teaching or preaching opportunity to show God's people the beautiful interconnections of Old Testament Scripture.

But how? Consider the sample text from the last chapter (Psalm 145). It is longer than the average psalm,[19] with the same general tone throughout. Chapter 6 noted that there is one widely recognized allusion (v. 8), two lesser recognized (vv. 3, 15–16), and one that was proposed in the last chapter (v. 18). While this might not always be the case, these four allusions—two in the first half of the psalm and two in the second half—provide structuring anchors for a sermon or lesson.[20]

Due to the structural primacy of blessing the Lord through praise in the psalm (vv. 1–2, 10, 21), I would structure the outline around *reasons to bless the Lord by calling out to him in praise*:

I. Reason 1: Because the next generation needs to hear about his greatness (vv. 1–7)[21]

II. Reason 2: Because his kingdom invites everyone to experience his grace (vv. 8–13a)[22]

III. Reason 3: Because he sustains all life and all who suffer (vv. 13b–16)[23]

IV. Reason 4: Because he is near when his people cry out to him (vv. 17–21).[24]

---

[19] Not counting superscriptions, the average psalm is 16.78 verses long.

[20] I realized this while listening to James M. Hamilton Jr.'s sermon on Psalm 103 (another somewhat encyclopedic and lengthy psalm). Hamilton used the allusion to Exod 34:6–7 in Ps 103:8 as an organizing centerpiece for the sermon. James M. Hamilton Jr., "Far as the East from the West," Kenwood Baptist Church, May 15, 2017, https://kenwoodbaptistchurch.com/sermons/far-as-the-east-from-the-west/. This demonstrates that even if there are not multiple allusions, they still can assist a homiletical outline.

[21] The allusion in this section occurs in v. 3, to Ps 48:1.

[22] The allusion in this section occurs in v. 8, to Exod 34:6.

[23] The allusion in this section occurs in vv. 15–16, to Ps 104:27–28.

[24] The allusion in this section occurs in v. 18, to Deut 4:7.

The goal is not to fully explain the three instincts in each of the psalm's four sections. Bryan Murawski cautions against preachers trying to give a full treatise on Scripture's use of Scripture but instead recommends they "be able to describe what the author is doing with the text he is doing it with."[25] The goal is to show listeners the rhetorical heartbeat of the text and how each source text serves that heartbeat.

The allusions can also provide guides to application for each section because they show how the Spirit-inspired writer applies texts.[26] In verses 1–7, the psalmist uses the words of another psalm (Ps 48:1) to tell of the Lord's greatness. Preachers and teachers might consider, then, showing listeners how to use the psalms in their homes to pray and pass on the knowledge of God. In verses 8–13a, the psalmist applies Exod 34:6 to the expansive nature of the kingdom of God. Preachers and teachers might consider encouraging listeners to expand their own thinking about who might enter Christ's kingdom through repentance and faith. In verses 13b–16, the psalmist applies a creation psalm (Psalm 104) to praising God's provision. Preachers and teachers might consider encouraging suffering or anxious listeners to envision themselves as one of those creatures the Lord mercifully feeds and satisfies. In verses 17–21, the psalmist applies Deut 4:7 to the activity of praise. Preachers and teachers might consider, especially as a sermon draws near to the closing hymn or a lesson nears the closing corporate prayer, encouraging listeners to trust that the Lord has promised to be near to the dependent cry of praise. While these are not fully orbed applications, they serve as a guide to applying the text.

Finally, and to conclude this book, drawing attention to the allusions in Psalm 145 when teaching or preaching conveys to God's people the

---

[25] Bryan Murawski, *Preaching Difficult Texts of the Old Testament* (Hendrickson, 2021), 207, 217.

[26] Question 3 under instinct 3, *What is the text's persuasive goal for the situation it addresses?*, becomes spadework with a view toward sermonic application.

stunning interconnectivity of the many sectors in Christian Scripture. The Psalms respond to Torah, and they work together to engender reliance on the Lord Jesus to whom "the Law of Moses, the Prophets, and the Psalms" bear witness (Luke 24:44–47). If this book has done what it set out to do, then may you find great joy and light in going "further up and further in" to the beauties of God's eternal Word.[27]

[27] C. S. Lewis, *The Last Battle* (HarperTrophy, 1998), 197–98.

Worksheet for Applying the Three Instincts

<table>
<tr><th colspan="3">Applying the Three Instincts to a Proposed Old Testament Allusion</th></tr>
<tr><td colspan="3">Alluding Text:
Source Text:</td></tr>
<tr><td>Instinct 1:
Terms</td><td>□ Rare Terms
□ Uncommon Phrases
□ Unique Clusters</td><td>Explain:</td></tr>
<tr><td>Instinct 2:
Themes</td><td>Both Immediate Contexts:</td><td>Both Broad Contexts:</td></tr>
<tr><td rowspan="4">Instinct 3:
Thesis</td><td colspan="2">1) How is the text arranged, and where does the allusion occur?</td></tr>
<tr><td colspan="2">2) What general human situation or spiritual condition does the text address?</td></tr>
<tr><td colspan="2">3) What is the text's persuasive goal for the situation it addresses?
□ Repent
□ Believe
□ Obey
Explain:</td></tr>
<tr><td colspan="2">4) How does the source text assist the alluding text in its persuasive goal?</td></tr>
</table>

ACKNOWLEDGMENTS

Many people deserve thanks for their role in this work. Many thanks to Paul House, who encouraged me to write a book like this. If I am one day half the Bible teacher this man is, I will be satisfied. Kristen Padilla deserves a mountain of gratitude for, during her time with B&H Academic, seeing the merit in a book like this, convincing her team of the same, and for her editorial expertise in bringing it to the present form. Many thanks also for the keen editorial improvements made by Renée Chavez of B&H Academic and Lindsey Tilghman, copyeditor.

I am grateful to Shawn Craigmiles, academic dean where I teach, for allowing me to develop an undergraduate course to pilot this book's concepts in the spring semester of 2023. The class would be more demanding than my normal Bible electives, so part of my recruiting tactic was to promise students who finished the course that their names would be mentioned in the acknowledgements of this book. Ten marvelous students answered the challenge. Ergo, I offer my gratitude to Abigail and Charles Swanson, Stephanie Clarke, Reva Godbolt, Seth Campbell, Kaelin Miller, Kaylin Brown, Jocelyn Royce, Kyle and Haylie Bowman. I was once asked about the best class session I ever taught, and my mind went straight to discussing 1 Samuel 17 with this group. It was a teacher's dream class roster. May the Lord continue to deepen your enjoyment of his Word!

This book was written in the crevices of weekly work and family life. Many thanks are due to my family for allowing me to recede into said crevices. My lovely wife, herself a professor and physical therapist, encouraged and guarded time for me to write. Thank you, Jackie, for your beauty, love, and support. And to my children—Hank the visionary, Eve the healer, and Cole the architect—thank you for being hilarious, sweet, and gracious. God is shaping each of you marvelously. I aspire to your enthusiasm, Hank; your empathy, Eve; your friend-making, Cole. Finally, I want to thank the Lord for making Scripture interesting. You could have made it boring. Thank you.

GLOSSARY

alluding text: a biblical passage containing an allusion (see chapter 1)

allusion: brief, intentional, recognizable references to another biblical text (see chapter 1)

broad context: the larger section of a biblical book containing a pericope, up to the whole biblical book itself (see chapter 3)

chiasm: an X-shaped Hebraic literary device wherein a center point is accentuated by the sections that flank it, which correspond in pairs (i.e., the first and last sections match, the second and second to last sections match, etc.) (see chapter 6)

collocation: refers to terms occurring together in a cluster (think co-location) (see chapter 3)

contextual awareness: evidence that an alluding text is aware of and potentially evoking elements of a source text outside of the terms involved in an allusion or quotation (see chapter 4)

diachronic: literally, "through time"; refers to exegetical investigations that focus or rely on the dating of texts (see chapter 2)

final form: the canonical form of biblical books after the process of writing and compilation is complete (e.g., when individual psalms reached their present form in the Psalter) (see chapter 2)

formal quotation: lengthy exact wording from a source text introduced by a citation formula; without the citation formula, sustained exact wording can still qualify an instance of Scripture's use of Scripture as a quotation but not a formal one (see chapter 1)

immediate context: the paragraph(s) or stanza(s) surrounding a biblical text (see chapter 3)

pericope: a self-contained passage of Scripture (see chapter 5)

rhetoric: the communicative pursuit of persuasive goals (see chapter 5)

rhetorical criticism (or rhetorical analysis): variously defined in biblical studies but in this book refers to uncovering how a source text serves the alluding text's persuasive goals for their readers (see chapter 5)

source text: the biblical text to which an alluding text refers (see chapter 1)

speech act: the active results sought or accomplished by the use of language (see chapter 5)

synchronic: literally, "with time"; refers to exegetical investigations that focus or rely on the literary relationships between texts (see chapter 2)

triconsonantal: refers to the nature of the Hebrew language deriving nouns, adjectives, and verbs from three-consonant root words; think "three consonants" (see chapter 3)

BIBLIOGRAPHY

Allen, Leslie C. *Psalms 101–150.* 2nd ed. WBC 21. Zondervan, 2018.

Anderson, A. A. *The Book of Psalms*. NCBC 2. Eerdmans, 1972. Repr., 1989.

Anderson, Bernhard W. "Exodus Typology in Second Isaiah." *Israel's Prophetic Heritage: Essays in Honor of James Muilenburg*. Edited by Bernhard W. Anderson and Walter Harrelson. Harper & Bros., 1962.

Armerding, Carl E. "Habakkuk." In vol. 7 of *EBC*. Edited by Frank Gaebelein. Zondervan, 1985.

Bail, Ulrike. "The Breath After the Comma, Psalm 55 and Violence Against Women." *Journal of Religion & Abuse* 1, no. 3 (1999): 5–18.

Bass, Derek D. "Hosea's Use of Scripture: An Analysis of His Hermeneutics." PhD diss., Southern Baptist Theological Seminary, 2008.

Bass, Derek D. "The Use of the Old Testament in the Old Testament: Reassessing Hosea 6:7 in Light of Hosea's Pervasive Use of Genesis." *The Law, The Prophets, and The Writings: Studies in Evangelical Old Testament Hermeneutics in Honor of Duane A. Garrett.* B&H Academic, 2021.

Beale, G. K. *Handbook on the New Testament Use of the Old Testament: Exegesis and Interpretation*. Baker Academic, 2012.

Beale, G. K., D. A. Carson, Benjamin L. Gladd, and Andrew David Naselli, eds. *Dictionary of the New Testament Use of the Old Testament*. Baker Academic, 2023.

Beetham, Christopher A. *Echoes of Scripture in the Letter of Paul to the Colossians*. BibInt 96. Brill, 2008.

Ben-Porat, Ziva. "The Poetics of Literary Allusion." *PTL: A Journal for Descriptive Poetics and Theory of Literature* 1 (1976): 105–28.

Berlin, Adele. "The Rhetoric of Psalm 145." In *Biblical and Related Studies Presented to Samuel Iwry*. Edited by Ann Kort and Scott Morschauser. Eisenbrauns, 1985.

Berlin, Adele, Avigdor Shinan, and Benjamin D. Sommer. *Psalms 120–150*. JPS Bible Commentary. Jewish Publication Society, 2023.

Block, Daniel I. *Judges, Ruth*. NAC 6. B&H Academic, 1999.

Block, Daniel I. "Will the Real Gideon Please Stand Up?: Narrative Style and Intention in Judges 6–9." *JETS* 40, no. 3 (September 1997): 353–66.

Block, Daniel I. "Recovering the Voice of Moses: The Genesis of Deuteronomy." *JETS* 44, no. 3 (September 2001): 385–408.

Blomberg, Craig. "The Structure of 2 Corinthians 1–7." *Criswell Theological Review* 4, no. 1 (1989): 3–20.

Blum, Edwin A., and Trevin Wax, eds. *CSB Study Bible*. Holman Bible, 2017.

Boda, Mark and Mary Conway. *Judges*. ZECOT. Zondervan, 2022.

Bradford, John. "Only Christ Brings Our Requests to God." *Psalms 73–150*. Vol. 8 of RCOS. Edited by Herman J. Selderhuis. InterVarsity, 2018.

Brown, Francis, Samuel Rolles Driver, and Charles Augustus Briggs. *Enhanced Brown-Driver-Briggs Hebrew and English Lexicon*. Electronic ed. Logos Research Systems, 2000.

Broyles, Craig C. *Psalms*. UBCS. Baker, 2012.

Calvin, John. *Commentary on the Book of Psalms*. Translated by James Anderson. Logos Bible Software, 2010.

Carroll, Robert P. *Jeremiah: A Commentary*. OTL. WJK, 1986.

Chapell, Bryan. *Christ-Centered Preaching: Redeeming the Expository Sermons*. 3rd ed. Baker Academic, 2018.

Charney, Davida. *Persuading God: Rhetorical Studies of First-Person Psalms*. Hebrew Bible Monographs 73. Sheffield Phoenix, 2017.

Chen, Kevin S. *Wonders from Your Law: Nexus Passages and the Promise of an Exegetical Intertextual Old Testament Theology*. IVP Academic, 2024.

Childs, Brevard S. *Isaiah: A Commentary*. OTL. WJK, 2001.

Connelly, Michael. *Crime Beat: A Decade of Covering Cops and Killers*. Little, Brown, 2006.

Connelly, Michael. *The Drop*. Little, Brown, 2019.

Connelly, Michael. *The Fifth Witness*. Little, Brown, 2011.

Connelly, Michael. *The Law of Innocence*. Little, Brown, 2020.

Connelly, Michael. *The Waiting*. Little, Brown, 2024.

Cook, Ryan J. *The Rhetoric of Praise: Prayer and Persuasion in the Psalms*. GlossaHouse Dissertation Series 6. GlossaHouse, 2018.

Cook, Ryan J. "Prayers That Form Us: Rhetoric and Psalms Interpretation." *JSOT* 39, no. 4 (2015): 451–67.

Cook, Stephen L. *Reading Deuteronomy: A Literary and Theological Commentary*. Reading the Old Testament. Smith & Helwys, 2015.

Davis, Ellen F. *Proverbs, Ecclesiastes, and the Song of Songs*. Westminster Bible Companion Series. WJK, 2000.

Dennis, Lane T., ed., *ESV Study Bible*. Crossway, 2008.

DeRouchie, Jason S. *Delighting in the Old Testament: Through Christ and For Christ*. Crossway, 2024.

Dettmar, Kevin. "*Dead Poets Society* Is a Terrible Defense of the Humanities." *The Atlantic*. February 19, 2014. https://www.theatlantic.com/education/archive/2014/02/-em-dead-poets-society-em-is-a-terrible-defense-of-the-humanities/283853/.

DiFransico, Lesley, "'He Will Cast Their Sins into the Depths of the Sea . . .' Exodus Allusions and the Personification of Sin in Micah 7:7–20." *VT* 67, no. 2 (2017): 192–93.

DiFransico, Lesley. "Identifying Inner-Biblical Allusion through Metaphor: Washing Away Sin in Psalm 51." *VT* 65, no. 4 (2015): 542–57.

Driver, S. R. *An Introduction to the Literature of the Old Testament*. Scribner's Sons, 1914.

Duguid, Ian M. "Introduction to Judges." In *CSB Study Bible*, edited by Edwin A. Blum and Trevin Wax. Holman Bible, 2017.

Eckel, Mark. *When the Lights Go Down: Movie Review as Christian Practice*. Westbow, 2014.

Edenburg, Cynthia. "How (Not) to Murder a King: Variations on a Theme in 1 Sam 24; 26." *SJOT* 12 (1998): 47–58.

Estelle, Bryan D. *Echoes of Exodus: Tracing a Biblical Motif*. InterVarsity, 2018.

Fantuzzo, C. J. "Acrostic." In *Dictionary of the Old Testament: Wisdom, Poetry & Writings*, edited by Tremper Longman III and Peter Enns. IVP Academic, 2010.

Fink, David C., ed. *Proverbs, Ecclesiastes, Song of Songs*. RCOS 9. InterVarsity, 2023.

Fishbane, Michael. *Biblical Interpretation in Ancient Israel*. Repr., Clarendon, 1988.

Flayhart, Bob, and Holly Mackle. *The Gospel Waltz: Experiencing the Transformational Power of Grace*. GCD Books, 2023.

Garrett, Duane, and Paul R. House. *Song of Songs and Lamentations*. WBC 23B. Zondervan, 2004.

Gerstenberger, Erhard S. *Psalms, Part 2, and Lamentations*. FOTL 15. Eerdmans, 2001.

Gibson, Jonathan. *Covenant Continuity and Fidelity: A Study of Inner-Biblical Allusion and Exegesis in Malachi*. LHBOTS 625. Bloomsbury, 2016.

Gladd, Benjamin L. "G. K. Beale and Benjamin Gladd—Dictionary of the New Testament Use of the Old Testament." Guilt, Grace, Gratitude Podcast. November 23, 2023. https://www.youtube.com/watch?v=P7eostbSNJ4.

Gladd, Benjamin L. "Keep Watch for Biblical Allusions." The Carson Center. July 25, 2024. https://www.thegospelcoalition.org/article/watch-biblical-allusions/.

Goldingay, John. *Psalms*. BCOTWP 2. Baker Academic, 2007.

Graves, Michael. *How Scripture Interprets Scripture: What the Biblical Writers Can Teach Us about Reading the Bible*. Baker Academic, 2021.

Gray, Rosie. "Trump Defends White-Nationalist Protesters: 'Some Very Fine People on Both Sides.'" *The Atlantic*. August 15, 2017. https://www.theatlantic.com/politics/archive/2017/08/trump-defends-white-nationalist-protesters-some-very-fine-people-on-both-sides/537012/.

Grogan, Geoffrey W. *Psalms*. THOTC. Eerdmans, 2008.

Gross, Max. "Seinfeld's 25 Greatest Contributions to the English Language." *New York Post*. July 1, 2014. https://nypost.com/2014/07/01/the-25-best-seinfeld-isms/.

Hamilton, James M., Jr. "Far as the East from the West." Kenwood Baptist Church. May 15, 2017. https://kenwoodbaptistchurch.com/sermons/far-as-the-east-from-the-west/.

Hamilton, James M., Jr. *God's Glory in Salvation through Judgment: A Biblical Theology*. Crossway, 2010.

Hamilton, James M., Jr. *Psalms*, Vols. 1–2. EBTC. Lexham, 2021.

Hamilton, James M., Jr. "The Skull-Crushing Seed of the Woman: Inner-Biblical Interpretation of Genesis 3:15." *SBJT* 10, no. 2 (2006): 30–54.

Hamilton, James M., Jr. *Song of Songs: A Biblical-Theological, Allegorical, Christological Interpretation*. Christian Focus, 2015.

Hamilton, James M., Jr. *Typology: Understanding the Bible's Promise-Shaped Patterns*. Zondervan Academic, 2022.

Harmon, Matthew S. and Gary Edward Schnittjer. *How to Study the Bible's Use of the Bible: Seven Hermeneutical Choices for the Old and New Testaments*. Zondervan Academic, 2024.

Hauser, Alan J. "Two Songs of Victory: A Comparison of Exodus 15 and Judges 5." *Directions in Biblical Hebrew Poetry,* edited by Elaine R. Follis, 265–84. JSOTSS 40. Sheffield Academic, 1987.

Hays, Richard B. *Echoes of Scripture in the Letters of Paul.* Yale University Press, 1989.

Henny, Ally. *I Won't Shut Up: Finding Your Voice When the World Tries to Silence You.* Baker, 2023.

Hill, Andrew E. *Haggai, Zechariah, and Malachi: An Introduction and Commentary.* TOTC 28. InterVarsity, 2012.

Hossfeld, Frank-Lothar, and Erich Zenger. *Psalms 3.* Hermeneia. Fortress, 2011.

House, Paul R. *1, 2 Kings.* NAC 8. B&H Academic, 1995.

House, Paul R. "God's Character in God's Word (Exodus 34:1–10, 27)." 2012 Biblical Studies Lectures. Beeson Divinity School. February 14, 2012. https://www.youtube.com/watch?v=fhxLc3owd9E.

House, Paul R. "Examining the Narratives of Old Testament Narrative: An Exploration in Biblical Theology." *WTJ* 67 (2005): 229–45.

House, Paul R. *Old Testament Theology.* InterVarsity, 1998.

House, Paul R., and Eric Mitchell. *Old Testament Survey.* 2nd ed. B&H Academic, 2007.

Hubbard, Robert L., Jr., and J. Andrew Dearman. *Introducing the Old Testament.* Eerdmans, 2018.

Hutchison, Daniel Allen. "Exodus in 2 Chronicles 10–36: An Exegetical Study on Inner-Biblical Allusion." PhD diss., University of Stellenbosch, 2021.

Jeffery, A. "Hebrew Language." *The Interpreter's Dictionary of the Bible* 2. Abingdon, 1962.

Kaiser, Walter C., Jr. *The Messiah in the Old Testament.* Studies in Old Testament Biblical Theology. Zondervan, 1995.

Kennedy, George A. *New Testament Interpretation Through Rhetorical Criticism.* University of North Carolina Press, 2014.

Kimelman, Rueven. "Psalm 145: Theme, Structure, and Impact." *JBL* 113, no. 1 (1994): 37–58.

Kirkpatrick, A. F. *The Book of Psalms*. Cambridge University Press, 1906.

Kreps, Daniel. "Ed Sheeran Wins 'Thinking Out Loud' Copyright Trial." *Rolling Stone*. September 25, 2023. https://www.rollingstone.com /music/music-news/ed-sheeran-not-liable-thinking-out-loud-trial -1234724464/.

Kselman, John S., and Michael L. Barré. "Psalm 55: Problems and Proposals." *CBQ* 60, no. 3 (1998): 440–62.

Kugel, James. "The Bible's Earliest Interpreters." *Prooftexts* 7:3 (1987). 269–83.

Kynes, Bill, and Will Kynes. *Wrestling with Job: Defiant Faith in the Face of Suffering*. IVP Academic, 2022.

Kynes, Will. "Beat Your Parodies into Swords, and Your Parodied Books into Spears: A New Paradigm for Parody in the Hebrew Bible." *Biblical Interpretation* 19 (2011): 276–310.

Lanier, Greg. *Old Made New: A Guide to the New Testament Use of the Old Testament*. Crossway, 2022.

Lanier, Greg, and William A. Ross. *The Septuagint: What It Is and Why It Matters*. Crossway, 2021.

Laurence, Trevor. "Serpent Seed and Son of God: The Enemy and the Imprecator in the Psalms of Vengeance." *CTR* 17, no. 2 (Spring 2020): 93–121.

Leonard, Jeffery M. "Identifying Inner-Biblical Allusions: Psalm 78 as a Test Case." *JBL* 127, no. 2 (2008): 241–65.

Leonard, Jeffery M. "Inner-Biblical Interpretation and Intertextuality." *Literary Approaches to the Bible*. Edited by Douglas Mangum and Douglas Estes. Lexham Methods Series Lexham, 2018.

Leonard, Jeffery M. "Identifying Subtle Allusions: The Promise of Narrative Tracking." *Subtle Citation, Allusion, and Translation in the Hebrew Bible*. Edited by Ziony Zevit. Equinox, 2017.

Lester, Brooke G. *Daniel Evokes Isaiah: Allusive Characterization of Foreign Rule in the Hebrew-Aramaic Book of Daniel*. LHBOTS 606. Bloomsbury, 2015.

Lewis, C. S. *The Last Battle*. HarperTrophy, 1998.

Liss, Hanna. "The Innocent King: Saul in Rabbinic Exegesis." *Saul in Story and Tradition*. Edited by Carl S. Ehrlich and Marsha C. White. Forschungen zum Alten Testament 47. Mohr Siebeck, 2006.

Longman, Tremper, III, and Peter Enns, eds. *Dictionary of the Old Testament: Wisdom, Poetry & Writings*. IVP Academic, 2010.

Luther, Martin. *Lectures on Genesis Chapters 31–37*. Luther's Works 6. Concordia, 1970.

Mackie, Tim, host. *BibleProject Podcast*. Classroom Sneak Peek: Jonah. Episode 3, "Hyperlinks and Patterns in Jonah." The Bible Project. September 6, 2021. https://bibleproject.com/podcast/hyperlinks-and-patterns-jonah/.

Mathews, Kenneth A. *Genesis 11:27–50:26*. NAC 1B. B&H, 2005.

Mays, James L. *Psalms*. Interpretation. WJK, 1994.

McCann, J. Clinton. *Judges*. Interpretation. WJK, 2002.

McCann, J. Clinton. "Psalms." In *New Interpreter's Bible* 3. Abingdon, 2015.

Meek, Russell L. *Ecclesiastes and the Search for Meaning in an Upside-Down World*. Hendrickson, 2022.

Melanchthon, Philipp. "Seeking Hidden Wisdom." In *Proverbs, Ecclesiastes, Song of Songs*. Edited by David C. Fink. RCOS 9. InterVarsity, 2023.

Miller, Patrick D. "Deuteronomy and Psalms: Evoking a Biblical Conversation." *JBL* 118, no. 1 (1999): 3–18.

Mitchell, Christopher W. *Song of Songs*. Concordia Commentary Series. Concordia, 2003.

Möller, Karl. *A Prophet in Debate: The Rhetoric of Persuasion in the Book of Amos*. JSOTSS. Sheffield Academic, 2003.

Moore, Carey A. *Esther*. Anchor Bible 7B. Doubleday, 1971.

Morrison, Craig E. *2 Samuel.* Edited by Jerome T. Walsh. Berit Olam. Liturgical Press, 2013.

Murawski, Bryan. *Preaching Difficult Texts of the Old Testament.* Hendrickson, 2021.

Nelson, Richard D. *Judges: A Critical & Rhetorical Commentary.* Bloomsbury, 2017.

Niditch, Susan. *Judges: A Commentary.* OTL. WJK, 2008.

Nogalski, James D. "Intertextuality in the Twelve." *Forming Prophetic Literature: Essays on Isaiah and the Twelve in Honor of John D. W. Watts.* Edited by Paul R. House and James W. Watts. JSOTSS 235. Sheffield Academic, 1996.

O'Connell, Robert H. *The Rhetoric of the Book of Judges.* Brill, 1996.

O'Donnell, Douglas S. "The Song of Solomon." *ESV Expository Commentary: Psalms-Song of Solomon.* ESV Expository Commentary 5. Crossway, 2022.

O'Dowd, Ryan P. *Proverbs.* The Story of God Bible Commentary. Zondervan, 2017.

Ortlund, Dane C. "'And Their Eyes Were Opened, and They Knew': An Inter-Canonical Note on Luke 24:31." *JETS* 53, no. 4 (2010): 717–28.

Paul, Larisha. "Ed Sheeran Plays Van Morrison Song as Proof He Didn't Steal from Marvin Gaye in Copyright Trial." *Rolling Stone.* May 1, 2023. https://www.rollingstone.com/music/music-news/ed-sheeran-references-van-morrison-copyright-trial-1234727230/.

Peterson, Eugene H. *Answering God: The Psalms as Tools for Prayer.* HarperSanFrancisco, 1989.

Phillips, J. B. *Your God Is Too Small.* Repr. Wyvern, 1957.

Philpot, Joshua M. "Was Joseph a Type of Daniel? Typological Correspondence in Genesis 37–50 and Daniel 1–6." *JETS* 61, no. 4 (2018): 681–96.

Piper, John. *Let the Nations Be Glad: The Supremacy of God in Missions.* 3rd ed. Baker Academic, 2010.

Robertson, O. Palmer. *The Flow of the Psalms: Discovering Their Structure and Theology*. P&R, 2015.

Ross, Jillian L. *A People Heeds Not Scripture: Allusion in Judges*. Pickwick, 2023.

Ross, Jillian L. "Type-Casting the Samson Family: Genesis Parodies in Judges 13–14." *JETS* 64, no. 2 (2021): 237–52.

Sailhamer, John H. *The Pentateuch as Narrative: A Biblical-Theological Commentary*. Zondervan, 1995.

Schmutzer, Andrew J. "Esther." *Ezra, Nehemiah and Esther*. Teach the Text Commentary. Baker Academic, 2018.

Schnittjer, Gary Edward. *Old Testament Use of Old Testament: A Book-by-Book Guide*. Zondervan, 2021.

Schultz, Richard L. *The Search for Quotation: Verbal Parallels in the Prophets*. JSOTSS 180. Sheffield Academic, 1999.

Selderhuis, Herman J., ed. *Psalms 1–72*. RCOS 7. IVP Academic, 2015.

Shalom-Guy, Hava. "The Call Narratives of Gideon and Moses: Literary Convention or More?" *Journal of Hebrew Scriptures* 11 (2011): 2–19.

Shepherd, Michael. *The Text in the Middle*. StBibLit 162. Peter Lang, 2014.

Smith, Suzanna. "Old Testament Rhetorical and Narrative Criticism." *Literary Approaches to the Bible*. Edited by Douglas Mangum and Douglas Estes. Lexham, 2018.

Sommer, Benjamin D. *A Prophet Reads Scripture: Allusions in Isaiah 40–66*. Stanford University Press, 1998.

Spawn, Kevin. *"As It Is Written" and Other Citation Formulae in the Old Testament: Their Use, Development, Syntax, and Significance*. de Gruyter, 2002.

Spencer, Samuel. "'Doctor Sleep': All the References to 'The Shining' Explained." *Newsweek*. November 8, 2019. https://www.newsweek.com/doctor-sleep-movie-shining-references-easter-eggs-stephen-king-stanley-kubrick-1470166.

Stanley, Christopher D. *Arguing with Scripture: The Rhetoric of Quotations in the Letters of Paul.* T&T Clark, 2004.

Strawn, Brent A. *The Old Testament is Dying: A Diagnosis and Recommended Treatment.* Theological Explorations for the Catholic Church. Baker Academic, 2017.

Stuart, Douglas. *Old Testament Exegesis: A Handbook for Students and Pastors.* 4th ed. WJK, 2009.

Swale, Matthew E. *From Recollection to Recommitment: The Rhetorical Function of Allusions to Judges in Psalms 68, 83, and 106.* BBR Dissertation Series 1. Gorgias, 2024.

Swale, Ryan G. "Delighting in the Love of the Bridegroom: The Song of Songs in Seventeenth-Century Scottish Spirituality." *Puritan Reformed Journal* 17, no. 1 (2025): 59–76.

Tanner, Beth LaNeel. *The Book of Psalms Through the Lens of Intertextuality.* StBibLit 26. Peter Lang, 2001.

Tate, Marvin E. *Psalms 51–100.* 2nd ed. WBC 20. Zondervan, 2018.

Tomasino, Anthony. *Esther.* Evangelical Exegetical Commentary. Lexham, 2016.

Tournay, Raymond J. "Les Relectures Du Psaume 110 (109) et l'allusion à Gédéon." *Revue Biblique* 105, no. 2 (1998): 326–31.

van Eijzeren, M. J. "'Halbnachts steh' ich auf': An Exploration into the Translation of Biblical Acrostics." MA Thesis, Utrecht University, 2012.

Van Pelt, Miles V. "Book of Song of Songs." *Dictionary of the New Testament Use of the Old Testament.* Baker Academic, 2023.

Van Pelt, Miles V. "Judges," *ESV Expository Commentary* 2. Crossway, 2021.

Vanhoozer, Kevin J. *Is There a Meaning in This Text?: The Bible, The Reader, and the Morality of Literary Knowledge.* Zondervan, 1998.

Wallace, Susan, ed. *A Dictionary of Education.* 2nd ed. Oxford University Press, 2015.

Waltke, Bruce K. "A Canonical Process Approach to the Psalms." In *Tradition and Testament: Essays in Honor of Charles Lee Feinberg.* Edited by John S. Feinberg and Paul D. Feinberg. Moody, 1981.

Watson, Larry. *As Good as Gone: A Novel.* Algonquin, 2016.

Webb, Barry G. *The Book of Judges*. NICOT. Eerdmans, 2012.

Westermann, Claus. *Isaiah 40–66.* OTL. WJK, 1969.

Wilkin, Jen. *Women of the Word: How to Study the Bible with Both Our Hearts and Our Minds*. 2nd ed. Crossway, 2019.

Wilson, Gerald H. *The Editing of the Hebrew Psalter*. SBL Dissertation Series 76. Scholars Press, 1985.

Young, E. J. *An Introduction to the Old Testament.* Eerdmans, 1989.

Young, G. Douglas. "The Language of the Old Testament." In vol. 1 of *EBC.* Zondervan, 1979.

Younger, K. Lawson. *Judges, Ruth.* Rev. ed. NIVAC. Zondervan Academic, 2021.

GENERAL INDEX

U

V

W

Y

Z

SCRIPTURE INDEX

Exodus

1 Samuel

2 Samuel